BE THE MENTOR WHO MATTERED

Minneapolis

First Edition 2025
BE THE MENTOR WHO MATTERED.
Copyright © 2025 by Colleen Stanley and LeAnn Thieman.
All rights reserved.

No parts of this book may be used or reproduced by any means, graphic, electronic, or mechanical, including photocopying, recording, taping or by any information storage retrieval system, without the written permission of the publisher except in the case of brief quotations embodied in critical articles and reviews.

10 9 8 7 6 5 4 3 2 1
ISBN: 978-1-962834-57-5

Cover and book design by Gary Lindberg

Praise for *Be the Mentor Who Mattered*

"This book is a must read for not only business leaders but really anyone that is looking to be a mentor. It's a masterclass in the quiet power of mentorship. Colleen and LeAnn don't just talk about the importance of guiding others, they show it through meaningful human, often unforgettable stories that span small towns, classrooms, boardrooms and hospital rooms. It's a beautiful reminder that we all have something to give."

Logan Eaton, Executive Vice President of Sales, National Land Realty

"After three influential books on sales, Colleen Stanley turns inward—and outward—with Be the Mentor Who Mattered, a timely, tender, and practical guide to answering the world's call for connection. With wit, warmth, and wisdom, she and LeAnn remind us that mentorship isn't just a business strategy; it's a human necessity. This book doesn't just teach you how to mentor; it inspires you to matter."

Jacyn Meyer, Instructor – Business School, University of Colorado Denver

"Having worked with Colleen for many years, I can attest to her drive, commitment, expertise, and authenticity in the world of sales and sales management. So, it's really no surprise that when Colleen turned her attention to her heart's work - mentorship- that she would knock it out of the park again. Centered in her work is the power of one-to-one relationships, regardless of their context (boss, coach, friend, etc). The message from Colleen and co-author LeAnn Thieman is simple: Share what you have to share, ask for what you need. *It's the doing that is hard.* This book offers a path to improve our ability to listen, learn and offer freely. Take the path..."

Chuck Smith, Executive Director, Chief Executive Network

"I believe everyone is created for greatness—I've always believed it. When I reflect on the role this belief has played in shaping mentorship in my life, I don't think about the formality of "mentorship." I think about the many people who brought out the best in me and this book reminds all of us that serving, loving and caring for others is powerful and it matters."

Julie Jackson, Senior Vice President, BSN Sports

"I was surprised—and delighted—that a sales powerhouse like Colleen chose to write about something as "simple" yet profound as mentoring. This book deeply resonated with me, sparking deep reflection and taking me down memory lane. I was reminded of the mentors who lifted me and mentees who gave me more than

I ever expected. Colleen and LeAnn have created a practical, powerful guide that will inspire you to help others through intentional, human-centered mentorship."

Mary Tafuri, Global Enablement Executive & Advocate for Human-Centric Leadership

"We've been taught at an early age to find a mentor, and to this day I continue to talk to my mentors…the ones who pushed me, molded me, guided me, and the ones who've just been an ear to listen. Colleen and LeAnn's new book pushed me to think more about my mentors and how I can continue to foster and enrich my connections with them. Enjoy and apply the wisdom and storytelling in this book."

Lauri Denison, Global Lead, Education and Development, Varian

"In my experience the most powerful mentorship often comes from peers invested in each other's success. We get to see this happen every day with our 45,000+ Vistage members around the globe who lean into our coaching and peer advisory platform. This book shows how "mentor moments" can spark anywhere- a question, feedback or encouragement- turning everyday interactions into opportunities to help others make better decisions. In a world that feels increasingly disconnected, Colleen Stanley and LeAnn Thieman deliver a timely reminder of the power of human connection."

Sam Reese, CEO, Vistage Worldwide

"I never thought I had the time or expertise to be a mentor. That is until MY mentor, Colleen Stanley, showed up early on in my sales management career. She modeled how important it was to develop others. (And at times was a tough love coach.) In this book, Colleen and LeAnn provide inspiration, comfort and confidence to step in and help others. What are you waiting for?"

Michael Kuehn, Learning and Development Coach/Denver Kids mentor

"Colleen and LeAnn call out the "elephant in the room" in our 21st century culture: In a hyper-connected world, people are lonelier, more distracted, and more disconnected than ever before. It's one thing to diagnose the problem. It's another to illuminate the path toward a solution. This is exactly what Colleen, LeAnn, and their fellow contributors do. With clarity, candor, and compassion, they remind us that mentorship, whether through a single word of encouragement or a lifetime of guidance, offers a positive way forward. This is a book needed at this moment.

John V. Miller, Esq., Executive Vice-President| Regional Manager Fidelity National Title Group

BE THE MENTOR WHO MATTERED

Colleen Stanley
and LeAnn Thieman

Wisdom Editions

Minneapolis

To my sister, Anne Marie Nelson.
Your day-to-day example of living a life of love, faith and generosity have inspired many. Thank you for the many times you've
shown up to love, support and encourage me.

Colleen Stanley

To my mom and dad, whose humble words of wisdom have guided me, and now others, for a lifetime.

LeAnn Thieman

Table of Contents

Introduction 1

**PART I: Why Mentorship Isn't Optional Anymore –
The Business and Social Case** 5

Chapter 1: Storm #1: The Breakdown of Community –
The Vanishing Village.. 7

Chapter 2: Storm #2: Social Media and Tech -
The Unintended Consequences 15

Chapter 3: Storm #3: The Pace of Change –
Too Fast to Process, Too Alone to Adapt 23

**PART II: The Mentors Who Molded Us –
What We Gained and Why We Give Back.** 31

Chapter 4: The Running Nun by Colleen...................... 33

Chapter 5: Show Up and Try by Colleen 35

Chapter 6: Words Make a Difference by Colleen 39

Chapter 7: It's Not So Bad by Colleen 43

Chapter 8: A Diamond in the Rough by Colleen............... 47

Chapter 9: It's Not Just a Numbers Game by Colleen 51

Chapter 10: It Only Takes One Conversation by Colleen....... 57

Chapter 11: The Golden Rule by Colleen 61

Chapter 12: A New Season by Colleen 65

Chapter 13: The Kick Butt Program by Colleen................ 71

Chapter 14: A Full Circle Moment by Colleen................. 75

Chapter 15: Two-and-a-half Cents by LeAnn 77

Chapter 16: A Bountiful Harvest by LeAnn.................... 81

Chapter 17: It's Time for Supper by LeAnn................... 83

Chapter 18: Light a Single Candle by LeAnn 85

Chapter 19: Wise People by LeAnn........................... 89

Chapter 20: I Can't; It Hurts too Much by LeAnn.............. 91

Chapter 21: Our "Stuff" by LeAnn............................ 93

**PART III: Mentors Who Molded Others –
Stories of Influence, Impact And Becoming** 95

Chapter 22: You Never Know by Nido Qubein 97

Chapter 23: She Didn't Let Me Off the Hook by Karen Short 101
Chapter 24: Attitude Adjustment by Jim Stanley 105
Chapter 25: This Is Me by Adenike Saliu 109
Chapter 26: What Am I Doing Here? by Allison Schmitt 113
Chapter 27: The Rookie and a Hundred Lessons by Chris Younger 117
Chapter 28: You Can Do This by Jerry Van Leuven 121
Chapter 29: You Don't Have the Full Picture by Sarah Kiley 125
Chapter 30: Resilient by Rolanda Pyle 129
Chapter 31: The Mentor Who Caught on Fire by Steve Spangler 133
Chapter 32: Be on Time, Be Ready by Matt Mitchell 139
Chapter 33: The 3 M's – The Mentors Who Made Me by Shiretta Shaw . . 143
Chapter 34: A Change of Perspective by Dave Hataj 147
Chapter 35: Flight Suit by Vernice "FlyGirl" Armour 151
Chapter 36: Year of the Ox by Lay Tin Ooi 155
Chapter 37: The Ripple Effect by Ginger Clayton 159
Chapter 38: The Power of One Person by Kanimozhi Sivakumaran . . . 163
Chapter 39: From Right-Hand-Man to CEO by Kent Stemper 167
Chapter 40: More than a Diagnosis by Martie Moore 171
Chapter 41: You Just Ask by Don Yaeger 173
Chapter 42: Lunch with the Legends by Stu Heinecke 177
Chapter 43: A Firm Handshake and the Lord's Prayer by Lori Jones . . . 181
Chapter 44: Now I Get It by David Sevick 185
Chapter 45: Take the Call by Erin Porteous 189
Chapter 46: Love and Giving by Val Gokenbach 193
Chapter 47: Find Your Wingman by Waldo Waldman 197
**PART IV: Someone Needs to Do Something –
From Intention To Impact** **201**
Chapter 48: Who Me? Yes, You. 203
Chapter 49: What Will Your Dash Say? 211
Chapter 50: Be the Next Greatest Generation 215
Acknowledgements 223
About the Authors 225

Also by Colleen Stanley

Growing Great Sales Teams. Lessons From The Cornfield.

Emotional Intelligence For Sales Success. Connect with Customers and Get Results.

Emotional Intelligence For Sales Leadership. The Secret of Building High Performance Sales Teams.

Also by LeAnn Thieman

Chicken Soup for the Nurses Soul
Chicken Soup for the Nurses Soul, Second Dose
Chicken Soup, Inspiration for Nurses
Chicken Soup for the Caregiver's Soul
Chicken Soup for the Father and Daughter Soul
Chicken Soup for the Mother and Son Soul
Chicken Soup for the Adopted Soul
Chicken Soup for the Grandma's Soul
Chicken Soup for the Soul, Answered Prayers
Chicken Soup for the Soul, a Book of Miracles
Chicken Soup for the Soul, Living Catholic Faith
Chicken Soup for the Christian Woman Soul
Chicken Soup for the Joy of Adoption
This Must Be My Brother
Balancing Life in Your War Zones
Adrift in the Storms
Self-care for HealthCare
Self-care for HealthCare, second edition
Self-care for HealthCare, third edition

Introduction

There are nearly one million books published every year so why would I write this one when my expertise and three other books focused on sales and sales leadership?

Not surprising, the first reason is to give an overdue thanks to the many great mentors who have molded me. As I look back, I clearly see how a few words of encouragement, one conversation or even on-going mentorship made a big difference in the trajectory of my decisions and ultimately, my life.

The second reason appeared during a conversation with Lois Creamer, a colleague and coach. I hired her to help me clarify my "why" for writing this book to guide future marketing and promotion efforts.

Lois asked compelling questions. Our discussion led me to share a few pages from my childhood. When I was fourteen, my beloved brother, John, a kind and charismatic young man, was killed in a car accident at the age of eighteen. He was loved by many, and his death devastated our family. It was the "straw that broke the camel's back." My parent's contentious divorce occurred about one year later and resulted in our family unit falling apart. No blame or bitterness, just one of the realities of this thing called life.

Lois stopped me. "Colleen, that's why you are writing this book. This is why you have so many vivid memories of people who stepped in, shared a kind word, or gave a helping hand. Your mentors filled an emotional void that your parents simply were not able to provide because they were grieving the loss of a marriage and a child."

It was a mic drop moment for me.

More than once, I'd wondered why I had so many mentor stories when many of my colleagues did not. As I've reflected on my life, I realized how often a mentor showed up at the right time, right place with the right words and direction.

Lois helped me discover my "why" is to encourage others to be aware of when and how they can fill a void for a person, even when the person isn't aware of that void.

The third reason for writing this book is to challenge the traditional view of mentorship. There are terrific books which outline formal mentorship programs, complete with goal setting, scheduled check-ins and feedback loops. There's nothing wrong with that approach, but for many, especially in small businesses that make up 99.9 percent of U.S. companies, it often makes mentorship feel like it's impossible to fit in on a packed schedule.

In my experience, powerful mentorship doesn't have to be formal to be powerful. One conversation, a mentor moment, can change the trajectory of a person's thoughts and actions. Sometimes it's a well-timed "I believe in you." Or it's a consistent example of integrity that quietly inspires someone else.

Other books and publications feature inspiring mentors behind world-famous figures, and those stories absolutely matter. But when mentorship is only framed through celebrity success, it can feel distant or exclusive. What about the small business owner who grew their company because of a neighbor's advice? Or the young manager who found their voice thanks to a colleague's quiet support? This book amplifies those stories, ones that don't make headlines but make a difference. I believe mentorship is for everyone because extraordinary change often begins with everyday people who show up, listen, and lead by example.

My definition of a mentor is simple: It's anyone who helps someone do better and be better. Call them role models, guides, teachers, coaches, colleagues, peers, parents or grandparents. The titles are different; however, the outcomes are the same: they made a positive difference in someone's life.

Mentorship isn't a new concept. Human beings have been shaping one another for centuries through storytelling, apprenticeship, and community. And yet, despite all the knowledge we have about the value of mentorship, too few people are actively engaging in it. I hope this book bridges the knowing versus doing gap, inspiring thousands to step up.

Everyone has something to contribute.

Which brings me to my co-author, LeAnn Thieman. We've been friends and colleagues for over fifteen years. We're both Iowa farm girls who were taught at an early age "to whom much is given, much is expected." When I shared my hope for this book, she wanted to contribute her tremendous storytelling skills developed while working for the Chicken Soup for the Soul company. It is her talent that brings the many stories of mentorship to life. And I might add, hours and hours of editing!

The Why Behind Each Section of This Book

Section one of this book is about the *why*—why mentorship matters now more than ever. We present the business and social case for mentorship in today's world, where community has frayed, social media and technology have rewired how we connect, and the accelerating pace of change has left many feeling anxious and alone. Helping one another isn't a luxury, it's a necessity.

Later chapters provide practical examples and guidance on *how* to mentor. But first, we begin with why the world is shouting for wisdom and why that call needs to be answered.

The second section is filled with personal stories of the mentors who molded LeAnn and me, shaping our values and actions.

The third section includes stories from individuals who have been the recipients of the heart and wisdom of mentors. They were excited to honor them and we hope their stories help you create your own.

The fourth section explores how to be a mentor. We'll guide you on discovering your talents, passion and wisdom, many of which you may not know you possess. You'll discover who, when, why and how you can serve others, regardless of your age, stature, location or season of life.

I close this introduction with the famous, somewhat time-worn starfish story. You've likely heard about the young girl throwing a few of the hundreds of starfish from the sandy beach back into the ocean. A passerby reminded her that she couldn't possibly save all of them. As she tossed another back into the sea, she said to him, "Well, I made a difference to that one." Soon the man and others joined in, and all the starfish were saved.

Thank you for reading this book. Find a starfish and be the mentor who mattered.

PART I
WHY MENTORSHIP ISN'T OPTIONAL ANYMORE – THE BUSINESS AND SOCIAL CASE

Perhaps you have seen or heard of the movie, The Perfect Storm. It's based on the true story of a fishing crew confronting the worst storm at sea during Halloween, 1991. Three raging weather fronts unexpectedly collided to produce a nor'easter and the fiercest storm in modern history. It became known as the Halloween Storm and then eventually "The Perfect Storm."

We're living in the perfect storm with multiple "weather fronts" hitting us, increasing the urgency and need for mentors.

The first is the breakdown in community. As people moved from rural areas to cities, traditional tight knit communities and the associated traditions---and mentoring---weakened. Informal mentorship---once found in breakroom conversations, church communities and family networks are fading, leaving a void to be filled.

Next are the unintended consequences from social media. In a desire to be more connected, people have become disconnected. Phones once attached to the wall are now permanent fixtures at the end of a person's arm. The comparison game has accelerated and so has depression and anxiety.

And finally, people are stressing out and burning out trying to keep up with the pace of change. It's like a perpetual game of whack-amole. When one skill is mastered, another pops up shouting, "you need to learn this." People feel behind or worry about being left behind.

In the next three chapters, we explore how these three forces call for each person to serve as a lighthouse, providing direction, advice and support.

Chapter 1
Storm #1: The Breakdown of Community – The Vanishing Village

The book *What Happened to You* deepened my understanding of the power and importance of community. Coauthored by Dr. Bruce Perry, a leading expert on trauma, and Oprah Winfrey, a shining example of a person who overcame adversity.

The book explores how early experiences shape our lives. One question Oprah asked Dr. Perry stood out to me: "How were our ancestors able to survive and thrive despite the fact that they faced plenty of trauma from plagues, wild animals, and loss of children due to lack of vaccines and medicine?" A good question since there were no mental health clinics, therapists, or hospitals.

His one-word answer: Community. Dr. Perry's research shows that one of the key ways people recover and rebound from trauma is through community. Our ancestors didn't survive on their own; they had elders, storytellers, and wisdom bearers to guide them.

My Community Saved Me

This research resonated with me because I grew up in a small Iowa farming town of 900 people. There are plenty of jokes about growing up in a small town. Everyone is "in your business or knows your business." Today, I am wise enough to say, "Hooray. Thank you for knowing my business, our family business." Because they knew all about us, people helped me through that dark time of my brother's death and my parents' divorce.

I lived in a "small tribe," surrounded by teachers and neighbors who knew what happened and offered support. My boyfriend's terrific family provided a safe place to hang out when things got tough at home. My church community provided me with faith that everything would somehow work out.

I didn't have to go it alone. My tribe watched over me and guided me.

There, I was exposed to my first role models of people helping people, especially during the annual harvest.

This time of year, farmers work eighteen-hour days, seven days a week, to "get the crops in." For city folks, think of "getting the crops in" as the equivalent of a company achieving year-end goals.

However, Mother Nature likes to send obstacles such as rain, snow, or even hail to interfere with achieving this goal.

Farmers overcome hurdles and delays because they don't go it alone. After achieving their goals, a neighbor calls a fellow neighbor still working in their fields. "We're coming over… we're going to help you get your crops in."

There's no mention of gas reimbursement, the cost of labor, or discussion around the wear and tear on their equipment. They recognize that if everyone receives help to achieve their goals, the town will thrive. Hard-working families earn more revenue for their families. There's more money for schools, hospitals, and churches.

Tom Brown, a sixty-two-year-old farmer from West Liberty, Iowa, was killed in a tragic UTV farming accident in 2023, leaving behind a wife and daughter. On top of this tragedy, there were crops to be harvested.

The West Liberty farmers showed up in full force to help the Brown family with the harvest:

- Ten combines
- Ten grain carts
- Sixteen grain-hauling semi-trucks

When I heard this story on the evening news, my eyes filled with tears and my heart filled with gratitude.

Tears of empathy for the family's loss.

Gratitude for West Liberty, Iowa farmers who understand the power of connection.

Tom Brown's daughter, Jessica Schroeder shared, "Community is everything."

Look around. How many people could use your help "getting their crops in?" How many people could use a helping hand to achieve a goal or overcome a setback?

The Breakdown of Community in Business

Planes, trains, and automobiles have created a transient society, moving people away from friends and family. The pandemic accelerated an increase in remote working, eliminating long commutes. For many employees, this was a welcome change. However, remote working has some unintended consequences.

Commutes decreased and, in many cases, so did the feeling of community. With fewer or no people in the office, informal hallway mentoring moments decreased. Grabbing a cup of coffee and conversations in breakrooms disappeared. Going to lunch with a colleague has been replaced with eating lunch by yourself while staring at a screen.

Engaging in after-work activities where you relax and build friendships has been drastically reduced. Gallup research has long shown that having a best friend at work is key to employee engagement, retention, and job success. That makes sense. However, deep friendships aren't formed through text messages or back-to-back Zoom meetings. They're built through in-person conversations that aren't rushed by the next item on the calendar.

As a young regional sales manager, I didn't know about this research but instinctively pushed for it. Each year, I'd make my case to the CFO to hold a summer regional meeting. Anyone who has planned a meeting knows the visible costs—airfare, lodging, food—all neatly recorded on the profit and loss statement. What doesn't get recorded are the invisible returns from a meeting: words of wisdom from a veteran to a new hire over dinner. Belly laughs with colleagues. Gaining confidence upon learning that you're not the only one facing challenges. And of course, that powerful sense of *I belong*.

I suspect this desire and push for meetings came from growing up in a small town where people knew each other's names and made time to visit. This didn't evolve because of a strategic planning session. It was a way of life. And maybe that's the lesson. In today's remote and hybrid work, building community isn't a nice-to-have, it's a cultural investment that pays off in loyalty, resilience, and joy.

The unintended consequences of the new workplace became clear when I was one of four guests on a business podcast. Three of us were in our late fifties to early sixties, and one was in her late twenties. The conversation turned to remote working. The "elders" in the group enthusiastically espoused this shift's benefits.

The young lady spoke up and presented another perspective. "Easy for all of you to work remotely. You've had the opportunity to form relationships and connections because of your many years of working in a corporate office. My age group wishes we could get access to executives with experience instead of having to figure out all this stuff on our own. I haven't even met my boss or any of my colleagues in person."

Gulp. A reality check.

Her comments were a wake-up call for the "elders" on the podcast. Remote working, with all its benefits, can be a community and connection killer. Today's leaders must be even more intentional about creating events and spaces to ensure we have a best friend at work.

The Breakdown of the Family Community

As Dr. Perry and Oprah explain in their book, our ancestors lived in tribes of often around 150 people. Having a group who knows, loves, and supports you is the key to thriving. Within these tribes, four to six adults were often present to raise children. These adults weren't always relatives; however, they were role models. They were there to discipline, nurture, and provide instruction. Today, often one parent is trying to raise two to four children. Their book states,

> "We expect a single working mother to be the one to throw the baseball with her eight-year-old, rock the newborn, read to the three-year-old and, by the way, cook a nutritious meal, help with homework, do the laundry, get everyone to bed, then wake up and get them all ready for childcare and school so she can go work all day, only to rush home to do it all again."

A study by the Pew Research Center of 130 countries and territories shows that the U.S. has the world's highest rate of children living in single-parent households.

Please don't close this book because you feel judged because of your status as a single parent, don't live close to your family, or are estranged from them. Don't shoot the messenger and miss the message: Parents need the help of mentors.

One of my nieces is a single parent, lives ten hours from immediate relatives, and has done a great job raising three active boys. All were involved in Boy Scouts and earned their Eagle Scout badges, which takes three to six years to complete all the requirements. This achievement only happened with the help of an experienced Scout or an adult leader. My niece didn't have to go it alone. As the late legendary basketball Coach John Wooden said, "It takes ten hands to make a basket." My niece had ten hands helping her.

According to research, youth with mentors are fifty-five percent more likely to enroll in college, and ninety percent more likely to become mentors themselves, creating a virtuous cycle of receiving and paying it forward. That is great news. And here's the not-so-great news. Sadly, thirty thousand children are on an eighteen-month waitlist at Big Brothers Big Sisters, waiting for that special person to show up. It's the knowing versus doing gap.

In my line of work, I teach, coach, and guide others, and I've been fortunate to receive messages from people who still use something they learned from a keynote or workshop I delivered. That's incredibly rewarding. But as I've studied mentorship more deeply, I realized I wasn't doing enough. So, when people reach out to me, some complete strangers, my answer is always an easy "Yes." It's one small step to closing the gap.

The Breakdown of the Church Community

Don't worry, I'm not trying to convert you. I'm simply stating facts. People don't attend church as much, and in the past, church communities provided a place of connection and relationships. It's where faith and people meet so they don't feel like they are going it alone.

An article by The Atlantic poses an interesting question. "Are Americans losing their ability to incorporate religion or any kind of intentional community into their lives?"

Jake Meador, the editor in chief of the quarterly magazine, *Me Orthodoxy*, notes in a recent survey that about forty million Americans have stopped going to church in the past twenty-five years. At its core, the issue is not just church attendance, Meador argues, but rather what our society has become:

> The problem is that many Americans have adopted a way of life that has left us lonely, anxious, and uncertain of how to *live in community*.

A Lesson from My In-Laws

When visiting my late in-laws, James and Elna Stanley, my husband and I would accompany them to their small, local church. The first time we attended, he and I did not practice what any good church teaches: Do not judge.

Nope, as we sat through the church service, we put on our big judgment hats. Why in the world did they attend this church? The minister was too old to be preaching. The singing was off-key and the interior of the church was sorely outdated.

Our judgment hats quickly disappeared as we mingled with the congregants in the church lobby. We "got over ourselves," recognizing that Elna and James joined this church because of one word: community.

This was not a mega church with talented singers, bands, or preachers; just a small church, populated by people who cared about one another. Crazily, it was like the popular TV show from the 80s and 90s, Cheers. The show's theme was about going to a bar, where "everyone knows your name." This church was like the Cheers bar, without Norm or alcohol of course.

Unhurried hugs were exchanged. True curiosity exhibited when asked about your health and well-being. Sincere concern expressed when asking about members of the family.

James and Elna were considered elders in the church. In our many visits, we heard stories about the advice and support congregants received from them. No formal mentoring, but tremendous role models of unconditional love and generosity.

Social Connections and Thriving

We are hard wired for connection. Look no further than the number of hit TV shows featuring the theme of community. Ted Lasso shows how an outsider coach built a cohesive team of champions because he "believed" in people and kindness. Seinfeld, a show about nothing, features four neurotic friends who accept one another, flaws and all. And Friends is all about the life of six friends navigating their way through work, love and heartache in New York City.

Why are people drawn to these shows? Community. Deep down we all need and want to belong to a group that includes us, loves us, doesn't judge us and supports us. In tough times, your community will help you reach the good times. Starting today, you can choose to help and guide others.

- ◊ Set a goal to help others "get their crops in." Make it a habit to ask people what they are working on and how you can help.
- ◊ Stop living as if the pandemic stay-at-home policies are still in place. Get proactive about creating your own group.
- ◊ Join a chamber, association or some type of group. The value of belonging to an association came full circle during the pandemic. My in-person work vanished overnight, and I had to pivot to virtual presentations fast. Thankfully, after over twenty years in the National Speakers Association, I had built relationships. Fellow speaker Brian Walters and his wife Karen not only sent me a shopping list for a home studio, but they also walked my assistant and me through the setup. *They helped me get my crops in.*

Like Tom Brown's daughter, Jessica Schroeder said, "Community is everything."

Chapter 2
Storm #2: Social Media and Tech –
The Unintended Consequences

In 1982, several people mysteriously died from taking Tylenol. Johnson and Johson executives swiftly acted, pulling the medicine from the shelves. Today, a similar crisis is going on because of the use and misuse of technology.

Jonathan Haidt, author of *The Anxious Generation: How the Great Rewiring of Childhood is Causing an Epidemic of Mental Illness*, shares that social media and technology are contributing to the rising mental-health issues among today's youth.

- The adolescent suicide rate has risen 167% for girls and 91% for boys since 2010, the year the smart phone with a front-facing camera was introduced.

- Depression diagnoses were up 145% for girls and 161% for boys.

But note, nothing has been pulled off the shelf!

Imagine having a conversation with an individual who spends six to eight hours a day drinking or doing drugs. We'd immediately say, "That person has a problem."

Ah, Houston, we've got a problem.

The average person in the United States spends four hours and forty-three minutes a day on their smart phone. For teenagers thirteen to eighteen, it's closer to seven hours per day.

Teachers try to limit the use of phones and are met with resistance from both the students and their parents. The response: "Sorry, we need to keep drinking!"

During an interview, author and speaker Simon Sinek shared provocative wisdom. "We don't give a sixteen year-old the keys to the car without a few driving lessons. Why do we think we can turn over this body of technology without instructions?"

We've handed the keys to technology without enrolling people in a "drivers ed" course. The digital native generation, born in the late 1990's and early 2000's, grew up with phones attached to the end of their arms and to their ears. Many never learned the "rules of the road" and it's causing a lot of accidents. We need more drivers ed teachers.

The Day I Fired a Client

It wasn't a typical client meeting where we discus new goals, progress towards goals, or troubleshooting issues. The agenda was to let a new client know I was firing them. It wasn't because invoices weren't being paid. It was because the sales team needed to be in a cell phone rehabilitation program, not a sales training program.

I'd conducted two workshops with this team and saw a pattern emerging. In each one, my multiple requests to remove cell phones were ignored. While engaging in role plays, their smart phones were in their line of sight, with the sales team responding at the first sound of a ding or ping. Now, this wasn't a seasoned team of salespeople who had mastered selling skills. This team wasn't exceeding their sales quota, so it was important for them to improve their selling skills.

"What's the reason you don't want to move forward?" asked the puzzled sales manager.

"You're wasting your money, and that's not the reason I'm in business. The team needs to develop focus skills before they are ready to master any other types of skills. No one learns when they are multi-tasking, and the team is highly distracted."

Silence. Then, "You're right. Thanks for your honesty. I inherited this team, and it looks like I have some work to do."

You might be thinking, well that's just that the next generation. Pandora's box is open, and it can't be closed.

Not true.

Two months earlier I had worked with a group of young sales professionals at PopSockets, the cell phone accessory company. At the time of the training, their business was exploding. I anticipated there would be pushback on our tech free training policy. There wasn't any. For two days, this group of young professionals were engaged and present. No cell phones. The difference was their sales leader, Bob Africa.

As he and I were debriefing the workshop and discussing next steps, I asked Bob, "What did you say to make your team so attentive? Did you threaten them?" Bob laughed and smiled, "No, I shared my expectations of their behavior and reminded them of the investment we were making in their personal and business development." An example of strong mentorship.

Courageous Leadership in a Swipe and Scroll World

It will take brave leadership, mentors, to set, model and reinforce productive and respectful behaviors to reverse the current behaviors we are seeing with those addicted to technology.

Dr. Howard Dover is one such leader. He is the director of the Center for Professional Sales at the University of Texas in Dallas. He understands the importance of preparing the next generation for success. Part of that preparation is teaching his students the need for and importance of being fully present. He has a no-cell-phones policy in his classroom. "I explain to my students that if I see someone looking at their cell phone, I will politely ask them to leave. I also share that my wife and I have a code if something is an emergency. In my twelve years of teaching, I've never received such a call."

Dr. Dover instilled this policy after hearing this true sales story. A senior account exec from a large CRM provider was at a business closing meeting. It was a big opportunity, so there were many representatives from the selling firm present to provide the image to the prospect that he would be supported by a big team.

As the senior account executive and the owner of the private company were discussing the final details, the buyer abruptly said, "Get out, I'm not doing this deal with your company." Unbeknown to the account executive, several of his younger colleagues had been using their phones throughout the meeting. "If your team can't pay attention to me when I'm about to sign a ten million contract, they surely won't pay attention after I've signed. I won't do business with your firm." And he didn't.

Obviously, these younger professionals desperately needed a drivers ed teacher.

Many years ago, my twenty-something-year-old assistant came into my office with a big grin. "You're going to be really proud of me. Last night, I was out to dinner with friends and asked everyone to put their phones in their purses. Initially they looked at me like I was crazy. But I shared what you teach in your emotional intelligence courses, that being present is one of the best presents we can give another person. So, I asked them if they wanted to exchange presents!" She went on to say how much more fun the evening was because she and her friends weren't distracted and were fully engaged in the conversation at the table.

This story made my day for a few reasons. First, I was proud this young assistant had embraced new relationship-building skills. Huge kudos to her for sharing this information and asking her peer group to consider another approach to catching up. Second, it reminded me that my insistence of tech-free zones during our one-on-one meetings and training workshops had made a difference. I was a drivers education teacher!

Can We Talk?

In the good 'ole days, employees used to walk into an in-person meeting with only a notepad and pen. They'd strike up a conversation with fellow colleagues, catching up on business and life. They were building trust, relationships and friendships.

A few years ago, I worked with a group of sales managers who flew in from all over the country for a two-day meeting. On the first morning, they arrived early—high-energy, high-performing, and laser-focused. But instead of using the time to engage with their peers, they immediately buried themselves in their laptops and phones, furiously responding to emails and texts. It was like watching a command-and-control center in action, except this wasn't a crisis, it was a meeting meant for collaboration. Beads of sweat formed on their foreheads as they prioritized firing off "one more message" over forging "one more connection."

Initially, I thought the group must have bonded over a nice dinner the night before. Nope, this was their first in person interaction in months. Instead of taking time to forge relationships, they defaulted to cleaning out their inboxes.

This scene plays out every day in corporate America, and it's a culture killer. Strong cultures aren't built through emails or Slack messages, they're built through conversations, one person at a time.

Fortunately, this group of smart sales managers was open to feedback. When I shared my observations, I saw a room full of nodding heads. They hadn't even realized what they were doing. It led to a good discussion on how their "one more message" behavior impacted their ability to lead a team. They had the answers. I only served as their guide, helping them discover that relationship building is the foundation of building trust, collaboration, and great teams.

Lack of connection and community is even worse during video meetings. In some cases, people don't turn on their videos. This is the equivalent of showing up to a meeting wearing a ski mask! It makes me wonder if the person is in a witness protection program. Or, is it a really, really bad hair day? Some just send their AI notetakers to meetings because they are too busy to show up, build relationships, and give support to their fellow team members.

We need role models who have the courage and self-awareness to bring back the good old days. Days where meetings required people to meet, greet, and converse with one another.

You've Got to Be Phubbing Me

A recent study conducted in Israel shows that young adults engaged in Phubbing, the act of ignoring someone in favor of your phone, is linked to lower empathy and less prosocial behavior.

We are a society of professional Phubbers! Has anyone besides me been in the middle of a conversation only to have the other person pull out their smart phone to check the latest ding? Suddenly, you're feeling rather foolish, talking to yourself! "Well, like I was saying…"

A few years ago, I was a member of a Vistage CEO group. It's a great organization which encourages peer mentoring *and* honest feedback. As part of the monthly meetings, we hear great speakers, one of which was Michael Allosso. He'd been awarded speaker of the year, so I was looking forward to his presentation.

A few minutes in, he stopped to address three participants. "Okay, you three have been on your phone since I started talking. I'm curious, is this the way you treat people during one-on-one conversations? Is this behavior present when conducting group meetings?" It was tough love mentorship as Michael called out the inappropriate behavior from the "cell-aholics" in the room. To their credit, the offenders thanked him for his honest feedback. And put away their phones.

We need more Michael's in the world. Role models who are willing to challenge people to be fully present and eliminate the illusion that they can multi-task.

In his 2024 annual letter to shareholders, Jamie Dimon, chairman and CEO of J.P. Morgan stated:

> "I see people in meetings all the time who are getting notifications and personal texts or who are reading emails. This has to stop. It's disrespectful. It wastes time."

All of us can be one hundred percent present in our conversations. Put your phones out of sight so you can see and hear the person right in front of you. Never make someone compete for your attention. Don't be a Phubber.

Look at Me

We've all taken a "selfie. I'm a selfie photographer in training, as my thumb usually appears in the first picture. There's nothing wrong with taking pictures. We've done it for years. However, the motive behind taking them has changed. Instead of capturing a great occasion or vacation to remember good times, the real motive is often to make sure everyone knows how great your life is. Our selfie culture is creating an increasingly narcissistic culture and higher levels of self-importance and self-absorption.

The irony is the more self-absorbed you are, the more depressed you become because you are:

- Absorbed in your problems rather than paying attention to other people's problems.
- Absorbed in making sure others know how successful you are rather than focusing on how successful you can make others.
- Absorbed in seeking approval rather than helping others feel like they belong.

In his book, *The Second Mountain. The Quest for a Moral Life*, David Brooks describes this behavior as hyper-individualism.

> The core flaw of hyper-individualism is that it leads to a degradation and pulverization of the human person. It is a system built upon the egoistic drives within each of us. These are self-interested drives—the desire to excel, to make a mark in the world, to rise in wealth, power and status, to win victories and be better than others. Hyper-individualism does not emphasize and eventually doesn't even see the other driver—the deeper more elusive moti-

vations that seek connection, fusion service and care.

Hyper-individualism erodes our obligations and responsibilities to others and our kind.

Walk into any bookstore and just try to find the "Other Help" section. You won't find it; however, you will find plenty of books in the self-help section.

It would behoove all of us to take a page out of High Point University. In his wonderful book, *Extraordinary Transformation*, President Nido Qubein shares how they've made service learning a core part of their curriculum. All incoming freshmen must complete at least fifty hours of community service per semester. In addition, they also created a required course in ethics which includes civic engagement. This can involve working with a refugee family, teaching children how to read, working in a homeless shelter or organizing cleanups in the city.

They are teaching the next generation how to be *other-absorbed* rather than *self-absorbed.*

Years ago, I was speaking at a national sales meeting. As part of the agenda, each regional office of the country chose a non-profit to support. Team after team got up, presented their project and shared what it meant to them. It struck me that they didn't need me as a motivational speaker, because each person in the room was deeply moved hearing stories from teammates who engaged in "other absorption work."

As we continue to navigate through the constant introduction of new tech tools and social platforms it's important for each one of us to think about how we can be a drivers ed teacher.

◊ Serve as a role model. Be fully present in every conversation.

◊ Create a no phubbers club at work and home.

◊ Pick up the phone instead of sending a quick text or email.

◊ Focus on being other absorbed, rather than self-absorbed.

Chapter 3
Storm #3: The Pace of Change – Too Fast to Process, Too Alone to Adapt

Bob Dylan's famous song, "Times Are a Changin'" pretty much sums up the pace of change in the day and age of technology.

> Come gather 'round people
> Wherever you roam
> And admit that the waters
> Around you have grown
> And accept it that soon
> You'll be drenched to the bone
> If your time to you is worth savin'
> Then you better start swimmin' or you'll sink like a stone
> For the times they are a-changin'

Today, many people feel like they are sinking like stones because of the pace of change. It's like taking a new mountain hike. You climb to the top thinking you're done, only to realize you have another *big* mountain in front of you to scale.

Ray Kurzweil, winner of the National Medal Technology and Innovation award shares valuable insights around the challenge of accelerated change.

> It is not the case that we will experience one hundred years of progress in the twenty-first century. Rather we

will witness on the order of twenty thousand years of progress—at today's rate of progress, that is.

Human beings simply can't keep scaling the mountains of change alone. Mountaineers in high-altitude expeditions rely on the expertise of sherpas. They guide climbers to the safest routes, navigate difficult and dangerous terrain, and help them adjust to high-altitude conditions to prevent sickness.

Like a sherpa, a mentor teaches others how to master and navigate new and difficult skills. They help people adjust to the pace of change to prevent the sickness of burnout and stress.

While our guides may not have experienced *this degree of change*, they have experienced change and the associated discomfort and doubt that accompany change.

Reverand Rohr, a Franciscan priest, author and blogger, shares the value of a guide. To paraphrase his many words of wisdom:

> A mentor is someone who companions and guides us through our Real Work, which is always going to be focused on the inside not the outside. They are the people of the future. Elders are tough, they've survived many struggles and many losses. They have survived economic collapse, social unrest, political struggles and great wars that have raged for years. Now, from their place of peace, they seek to send their wisdom into our hearts, to guide us to reconciliation, to show us our mistakes before we make them.

They have scaled mountains and can help others do the same.

The Gift and Burden of Technology

Change used to happen at a slower pace. Just look at the evolution of the telephone.

Antonio Meucii, an Italian innovator, is credited with inventing the first basic phone in 1849. In 1854 Alexander Graham Bell won the first U.S. patent for the device. The first telephone line was constructed during 1877–1878. We started communicating with the candlestick phone during 1920–1930. Fast forward to 1992, and the first smartphone was invented.

We had a full 143 years to adapt to the changing dynamics of the technology of the telephone.

Can you imagine any product or company surviving today if it took that long to evolve and adapt? Today, people and companies must learn to quickly adapt or fail.

Writer and biochemist Isaac Asimov shares, "The saddest aspect of life right now is that science gathers knowledge faster than society gathers wisdom."

Dr. Nadya Zhexembayeva is the founder of the Reinvention Academy. Her research shows that every fifth organization in the world is reinventing itself every twelve months or less. "Gone are the days when you support a one-time transformation, and things will go back to normal for a few years." Times they are a-changin.'

For years, I've preached that it takes a sales village to win and retain business. Now, my sermon has changed. It will take a village of mentors to help all of us keep up with the pace of change.

Connections and Collaborations

The Vagabonds are a great example of successful businesspeople who understood the power of community and collaboration to stay ahead and manage change. The Vagabonds were a group of men: Henry Ford, Thomas Edison, Warren G. Harding, and Harvey Firestone. These twentieth-century economic powerhouses created a mobile mastermind group, famous for taking their cars on long road trips together, usually led by Henry Ford and Thomas Edison. Hence, the name Vagabonds.

They'd spend weeks out on the road, without any of the distractions of their businesses where they could discuss any topic they wanted. They shared their successes, failures and sought advice from one another.

This group of accomplished individuals served as sherpas to one another. They collaborated and took time to build relationships which were vital to their success.

> *We need more "Vagabond groups" in our personal and professional lives.*

Ironically, when we are running fast and furious on the change treadmill, the very things that help us to connect and collaborate take a back seat! We're not taking enough road trips.

LeAnn was instrumental in creating a Vagabond group. She owns a beautiful cabin surrounded by tall Evergreen trees and a bubbling creek. For more than fifteen years, she's invited a group of speakers who take a road trip to her cabin. We enjoy cups of coffee, way too much food and a whole lot of great conversations. Over the years, we've offered business advice and support to one another. We've delighted in the birth of new babies or grandbabies. Hugs and tears have been exchanged upon the death or loss of a loved one. Strong shoulders to lean on have been available when one of us is going through a difficult time dealing with an aging parent or difficult teenager. We slowed down to build community and connections. It's peer mentoring at its finest.

LeAnn and I brought two different perspectives and opinions in collaborating on this book. Our expertise is in two different areas, mine being sales and LeAnn's being healthcare. However, because of the years invested in building a relationship, we were able to disagree, agree and in the end come up with better ideas for this book.

It's easier to collaborate when you take the time to know a person, because you understand and trust his or her intent when debating on new ways to achieve goals or solve problems. In our busy world, we must remember there's no shortcut to building friendships and relationships.

The Antidote to Knowledge Overload

Brandon Nye is a successful vice-president of sales for InMode. They provide innovative medical devices for minimally invasive cosmetic treatments. One of the reasons for his success is the philosophy instilled in his sales team: You don't have to go it alone. When we spoke, he shared, "We help one another achieve goals, especially the senior salespeople. My team is sending messages and calls all day, answering questions or giving advice." He further emphasized the need for elders on sales teams to help new or young professionals succeed. Peers guiding peers. Brandon's team isn't trying to climb the mountains of change alone, because his team is equipped with sherpas. He's created a Vagabond group.

Several studies and reports indicate that the average person today processes as much as seventy-four gigabytes (GB) of information daily. To put that in perspective, that's like watching about sixteen movies. Roll back 500 years ago and seventy-four GB of information would have been the total amount a highly educated person would consume over their entire lifetime! Do we really think we can get by without the help of others given this information?

A few years ago, I spoke in Murano, Italy. (Have you noticed I don't mention my Brookings, South Dakota engagements?) After a day of working with sixty global sales managers, we enjoyed a group dinner. I sat next to a very bright, seasoned engineering manager. As we got to know each other, he shared his concerns about remaining relevant. "I've been doing this awhile; however, everything is changing so fast it makes me wonder how I can learn everything I need to know so I don't get left behind."

The pace of change was creating self-doubt. It was burning and stressing him out. I regret that I didn't ask more questions about his support system. Who and where did he turn for advice and encouragement? Was he going it alone? Did he have any guides? I missed an opportunity to be a sherpa.

Holy Batman

Batman and Robin are one of the most iconic duos in pop culture, not because they were alike, but because they weren't. Batman, shaped by trauma and justice, was the brooding strategist. Robin, younger and more optimistic, brought levity, energy, and a fresh perspective. Together, they made each other better.

A few years ago, I worked with a dynamic duo. Robert, a successful sales producer in the property and casualty business, had a huge book of business leaving limited time to prospect for new business. Raymond, his protégé, an energetic, smart, twenty-something-year-old had a steep mountain to climb, learning product knowledge and selling skills.

It was a match made in heaven. Raymond prospected for new opportunities and taught Robert the latest tech tools to shorten research and prep time. He uncovered new leads, keeping the sales pipeline full. In turn, Robert taught Raymond storytelling skills, how to deal with objections and ask compelling questions to connect with C-suite executives.

This is the heart of peer and reverse mentoring. It's not just about passing wisdom down, it's about creating a two-way street where young and old share expertise and experience. This is how we will stay ahead in an ever-changing world.

Why Is Everyone Quitting?

In a 2021 study, McKinsey asked managers why employees were quitting. They thought it might be due to seeking more pay. However, the data showed that employees were leaving because they didn't feel recognized and valued by their managers or organization.

Eric Chester, author of *Fully Staffed*, shares provocative insight. "Every mentor is a leader. But not every leader is a mentor."

So, what's going on? Have companies suddenly promoted people to leadership roles who don't care about people? Are they running ads that say, "Looking for people who don't like people." I don't think so. I suspect this lack of recognition and not feeling valued goes back to the pace at which people work. I know because a few years ago I had a "wake-up call."

In one day, I had three members of my team begin their conversations with, "I know you're busy." Unknowingly, I was sending a message to my team that I didn't have time for them, which impacted the quality and quantity of conversations. With my new self-awareness, I ripped off the busy badge from my jacket and decided to give them the time and attention they deserved.

Organizations are filled with overscheduled human beings which dramatically impacts retention and time to mentor.

- **Overscheduled** people don't have time (or take time) to show recognition or appreciation. They get right down to business or the problem at hand neglecting the importance of showing people they are valued for their large and small contributions.

- **Overscheduled** people develop the skill of partial attention. They pay attention to half the conversation because they are thinking about their next meeting, one that is tightly scheduled right after this meeting. Mary Kay Ash, founder of Mary Kay Cosmetics said, "Pretend that every single person you meet has a sign around his or her neck that says, make me feel important." Overscheduled people don't make anyone feel important.

- **Overscheduled** people can't demonstrate empathy, a powerful communication skill. Hurry is the enemy of empathy and it can't be demonstrated when a person is hurried and harried. As a result, the basic human need to be heard or understood is not met.

You can be the person that steps in to fill the leadership gap created by our overscheduled, rushed society.

Calling all Wise Leaders

Faster learning occurs when we have access to people who can short-cut our learnings. It will take wise leaders to realize that we need to slow down to speed up.

It's simple math. Slow down and give:

- **Thirty minutes** of undivided attention and coaching to shorten a person's learning curve.
- **Thirty minutes** of side-by-side teaching. Show someone how to do the task rather than just tell them to do the task. It decreases mistakes and increases productivity.
- **Thirty minutes** of encouragement. Be that best friend or elder at work.

Technology is accelerating change and will do great things for our world. I can still remember driving to appointments with one hand on the wheel, the other looking at a map. Talk about distracted driving! Or calling in orders from a pay phone. (Look it up on the internet.)

Times they are a-changin.' We need a village of mentors to keep up with the pace of change.

- ◊ Think about how and where you could be a sherpa for another person, young or old.
- ◊ Create a personal and professional Vagabond group. Take a road trip.
- ◊ Examine your calendars to see where you are overscheduled and not providing much needed mentorship.

PART II
THE MENTORS WHO MOLDED US –
WHAT WE GAINED AND WHY WE GIVE BACK

LeAnn and I are living proof of the power of mentorship. We are who we are today because of the mentors who came into our lives—for a reason, a season, or in some cases, a lifetime.

Some of these mentors shaped us in an instant, offering a few words that dramatically shifted our self-image or reframed a situation. We call these "mentor moments"—brief encounters with lasting impact.

Others influenced the course of our careers or personal development through a single, pivotal conversation. Then there are those who walked alongside us over time, investing hours, generously sharing their wisdom, experience, and belief in our potential.

Not every mentor used words. Some taught us simply by how they lived. Their actions spoke volumes, and we learned by observing the way they treated people, faced adversity, or stayed true to their values.

In Chapters 4 through 14, you'll read Colleen's mentoring stories followed by Chapters 15 through 21 which feature LeAnn's stories.

We are grateful to share these stories of people who impacted our lives. We hope they spark memories of your own mentors—and perhaps inspire you to become one for someone else.

The Mentees

Chapter 4
The Running Nun by Colleen

It was recess. We fourth grade girls and boys were huffing, puffing, and laughing and racing as hard as we could trying to keep up with the lead runner... Sister Emma in her full nun habit.

As our first through eighth grade Catholic school principal, she was a fun "out of the box" thinker. Sister Emma was the first nun at our local convent to don the new apparel, which eliminated long robes and scapulars. And she was a good salesperson; she knew her target audience. Our young minds responded to the lively new hymns she played on the piano, replacing what we thought were boring, traditional ones. Today, we'd call her an "early adopter."

And Sister Emma was a committed educator, insisting her pupils weren't going to miss opportunities for learning. Our small school didn't offer shop classes, home economics, or gym for physical education, however the local public school did. Somehow, Sister Emma persuaded that principal to allow Catholic school pupils to join these classes.

But there was one small problem. The school buses were not available during the day, and we needed transportation to the public school on the other side of town.

No problem for Sister Emma. She purchased a used hearse and took out the seats. "Jump in!" she beamed as she waved ten of us in to sit on the floor. I can only imagine the looks on people's faces as they passed a nun driving a hearse filled with a bunch of kids. I'm fairly certain the word "Jesus" was uttered more than once, and not in the form of a prayer.

Sister Emma taught me:

Get comfortable thinking outside of the box. When I authored my second book, Emotional Intelligence for Sales Success, I had quite a few naysayers. "No one in the sales profession is going to buy a book on soft skills. The title isn't catchy enough." Fortunately, I ignored them because Sister Emma whispered in my ear. "Go for it. Run the race, sing a new tune, and drive a different vehicle to success." That book exceeded all expectations and is now published in eight languages.

Where there is a will, there is a way. Many times in my life I didn't know how to accomplish something. However, I always figured it out, often with the help of mentors. I think the many rides in the hearse across our small town were teaching moments in disguise, one where the young riders were learning, "where there is a will, there is a way."

Chapter 5
Show Up and Try by Colleen

"Okay, ladies, four steps to the right. No, your other right!" our instructor shouted with a laugh. It was evident that many of our potential drill team members had never taken a dance lesson.

The town had been buzzing with excitement, welcoming our new football coach, Dick Gruber, and his wife Jan, the new Spanish teacher. We quickly learned that Mr. Gruber's easy smile and jovial demeanor was not to be confused for lack of competitiveness. We knew he was going to put the West Bend Bulldogs on the map. Little did anyone know that Jan Gruber, with her jet-black hair and jet-fueled energy, would also create a winning team.

Jan showed up to teach Spanish AND create the school's first dance/drill team. Not the easiest goal to achieve. But Jan was not deterred by our lack of experience and, in many cases, our lack of rhythm.

A combination drill instructor and comedian, she was my first example of engaging in perfect practice. In our small gym, Jan broke down each dance routine step by step, no guessing or assuming the right move. Excellence was expected and accompanied by a good sense of humor.

Our community enthusiastically embraced the new drill team during half-time performances, loudly clapping and snapping pictures. We felt like rock stars in a band.

However, Jan wasn't satisfied with performances to the hometown crowd. She decided we were ready for the big time and enrolled us in the very first Iowa State Dance and Drill Team tournament. Since this was the first, there was no division of competition based on school size. Little West Bend High School would be competing against schools three to four times our size.

Once again, Jan was not dissuaded.

Competition day came, and sixteen excited girls boarded the orange school bus in our velveteen purple dance dresses with white puffy sleeves and polished white tennis shoes. And I'd be remiss not to mention our iridescent blue eye shadow.

147 miles later, we exited the bus in Vermillion, South Dakota. We walked into the huge gym, and awe, terror and self-doubt swallowed us as we watched competitors with much larger teams stride in. They were poised and polished... none wearing iridescent blue eye make-up. Our team seemed to get smaller and smaller.

Jan clapped her hands. "Girls, don't let them intimidate you. We may be small, but we are mighty. Mighty new at this, but we can do this! We aren't underdogs, we're super dogs!" Her reassuring demeanor, humor and confidence calmed our nerves. "Do your best and have fun!"

When it was our turn and the music started, we did just that. The hours and hours of rehearsals paid off as we danced our hearts out.

At the end of the exhausting, exhilarating day, the sixteen of us held hands and our breaths as the results were announced. I don't remember the competing school names; however, I remember the moment.

"Third place–ABC High School." *Well, that makes sense. They've had a drill team for years. Darn, I hoped we might have a shot at third place.*

"Second place–XYZ High School." *Not surprising. Their school is four times larger than ours.*

"First place–West Bend High School."

We all stood statue-like, looking around. Surely the announcer had made a mistake. He repeated louder, "First place, West Bend, Iowa." All sixteen of us stormed the floor, grabbed the trophy, and raised it high in the air with tears of joy. There was blue eye make-up all over the place.

Jan taught me:

You don't have to be big to win. This high school experience helped me when I took my first sales job at Varsity Spirit Corporation. When I joined, the company was the David in the David and Goliath fight. The competition was about eight times larger in revenue, employed dozens more salespeople, and had much better name recognition.

Jan's influence, as well as my youth and ignorance, helped me fearlessly go up against the Goliath. I wasn't worried that Varsity was the smaller underdog because Jan had taught me how underdogs can become super dogs. Today, Varsity is the largest company in the world in their industry. I worked for them for ten years, and I attribute the beginning of this great career to the lessons taught by Jan.

You don't have to be big to win. You do have to show up and try. And while you are showing up, do your best and have fun.

Sometimes you discover a talent you didn't know you had. Jan Gruber took a group of sixteen gangly, giggling, inexperienced girls and made us superstars. She modeled the importance of showing up and trying, often before you know what the heck you are doing. This philosophy---and mindset---created more than one opportunity for me.

- In the 80s, I "showed up" and auditioned to be on the Jazzercise national training team. I had no experience in training and speaking, however, because of Jan, I did have experience in showing up and trying. To my surprise and amazement, I was selected and traveled the country certifying new Jazzercise franchisees. This opportunity taught me that I had a love and gift for teaching.

- In the 90s, I resigned from my role of VP of Sales at Varsity to try my hand at full-time teaching and speaking about sales. I moved to Denver, Colorado, where I had no experience or business contacts. During the first few difficult years, Jan whispered in my ear more than once. "Show up and try." Fast forward to 2024, I was recognized as the number one Top 30 Global Sales Guru, all because I showed up and tried and discovered a talent I didn't even know I had.

Chapter 6
Words Make A Difference by Colleen

"Just a small town girl!" I belted at the top of my lungs as I cruised down the highway in my old Malibu Classic car packed to the ceiling with all my belongings. College graduation complete, grand ideas filled my head as I drove to Minneapolis, Minnesota. With the windows down and the wind in my hair, I sang along with Journey, "Don't stop believing." Life was good.

Three excited young friends and I shared an apartment ready to begin our post college careers. There was only one small problem... we had no jobs or rent money. No helicopter parents hovered around offering to pay for rent and food until we found work. It was a different time.

Sitting at our yard-sale kitchen table, I combed newspapers day in and day out looking for a job. New in town, I often got lost driving to interviews. I quickly learned how to read non-verbal and verbal cues as the human resource director frowned while reviewing my resume filled with waitressing experience. "Hmm. Interesting." And because I didn't know how to prepare, I heard no's, not yes's.

Time was ticking. Cash saved from my college part-time job was running out and food in our kitchen cabinets running low.

Finally, I landed a job at the American Cancer Society as the executive assistant to the state fundraising director, Carol. This five-foot-four woman accomplished more in one day than most people do in a week. She could persuade donors to give time and money when they had little of either. Without knowing it, I was exposed to my first professional salesperson and a great one at that.

Carol and I met for our weekly meeting in her inspirational office filled with motivational quotes, awards and thank you notes from grateful recipients of the organization's dollars. Half-way through the meeting, she paused and said, "You know, you are one of the most organized assistants I've ever had."

"Uh, no, I'm not organized," I blurted. I was that little kid who left mittens, stocking hats and coats behind at school or school events. My rightfully frustrated parents repeated, "You'd lose your head if it wasn't attached." My translation? I'm disorganized.

Carol laughed and reiterated. "No, you are an organized person. And let me tell you why." She went on to list the many things I'd done to structure her days and projects.

It was a mentor moment.

Maybe I am organized, I thought to myself.

Maybe losing things should be attributed to being distracted not disorganized.

Carol taught me:

The power of positive self-talk. I attended my first-time management course while working at The American Cancer Society. Because of Carol's words, I showed up to the course with pen and paper in hand, prepared to learn. My former self-limiting beliefs about being disorganized were gone. The new me showed up confident and eager to learn new skills.

The power of words. Carol taught me the power of words in a conversation, and I was fortunate to be able to take her advice and pay it forward many years later.

A young lady I'll call Sarah, a ward of the state, lived at The Tennyson Center for Children due to the abuse she endured at home.

As a volunteer, I met with her once a week and often our meetings included a trip to the local Chipotle. (Sarah loved Mexican food; I should have purchased stock in Chipotle for the amount I ate that year.)

Sarah was shy and lacked confidence in her decision-making abilities due to her difficult background. The first time we went out, she turned to me and whispered, "Will you order for me?"

I was about to do so when Carol's words popped into my head, the ones that changed my self-limiting beliefs. Channeling my inner Carol, I smiled and put my arm around her shoulder. "Sarah, you're a smart girl. You know what to order." She looked at me, nodded, took a breath and ordered. From then on, she slowly built her confidence in making decisions and speaking up.

A couple of years later, at a volunteer appreciation event, the volunteer coordinator read a letter from Sarah. "Thank you, Tennyson Center, for helping me get set-up for a better life. And thanks to Colleen because she always told me I was a smart girl." I gulped; tears filled my eyes as I realized that Carol's mentor moment had been paid forward. Words matter.

Chapter 7
It's Not So Bad by Colleen

After a couple of really good years at the American Cancer Society, I married my college sweetheart and his job as a Josten's sales representative took us to Omaha, Nebraska. He was busy selling class rings, graduation accessories and awards.

I was on the hunt for my next role and landed a position as a merchandiser for a small chain of retail stores in the Midwest called The Half Price Stores. The business model was similar to the many off-price chains we see today with T.J. Maxx, Marshalls or Burlington.

My title of merchandiser may sound glamorous; however, I quickly learned it was a fancy name for being a professional order tracker. On more than one day, I felt like I had a starring role in the show Bounty Hunter, tracking down "vendor fugitives" that were not shipping goods on time.

My skills were put to the test when we were opening a store in Kansas City. We had a full-page ad running, one of which featured a special buy on Levi jeans. These were the "hot retail" item at the time. The New York City vendor continued to tell me, "Trust me, the jeans have shipped." However, they couldn't provide me with the appropriate shipping data. He was lying and had me running around in circles. "What am I going to do to get these jeans shipped? What happens if they miss the store opening? Will I get fired?"

I bounced around ideas. Maybe I should rent a U-Haul and drive to the east coast? Hire Guido to show up at the vendor's location with a threatening message?

The store opening grew closer and closer. The Levi jeans were nowhere in sight. I was burning up phone lines and burning up inside with the stress and fear of these jeans not making it to the grand opening.

Finally, the day before the store opening, the jeans finally arrived in our warehouse located thirty minutes from our buying office. I expedited the order, personally walking the jeans through the warehouse, constantly touching them for fear they would disappear. Because of the late arrival, we had to load the merchandise on a Greyhound bus. I didn't take my eyes off of these prized goods and closely supervised the loading of multiple boxes onto the bus.

I cannot remember why the shipment of jeans didn't make it to the store opening. I don't recall if they got lost in transit or the bus simply arrived too late. What I do remember is the dread of telling the big boss, Stan, of the missed shipment of goods that were advertised but nowhere to be found in the store.

I summoned my courage and set up a meeting with him. Stan was a tough merchandiser and sported a "resting business face" every day. I cleared my throat and began reviewing everything I'd done to ensure the timely arrival of these jeans. "Here's the documentation of phone calls. This is the timeline for expediting the merchandise through the warehouse. Oh, and here is the receipt from the Greyhound Bus service."

I was out of breath and waited with bated breath for Stan's response.

Stan's head was down, writing notes. When he finally looked up, lowered his glasses and made only one statement, "Sounds like you didn't get the job done." Then he went back to writing more notes.

Not exactly the sandwich method of giving feedback where the boss shares something positive that you did, an area for improvement and wraps it up with another positive.

This was you failed. End of story. No sandwich.

Tears stung my eyes as I made my way back to my office. I held my head in my hands, going over and over all the steps I had taken to ensure a timely delivery. I dug through my piles of notes one more time, looking for any oversight on my part.

Stan's response wasn't fair. It was terse with no credit given for the effort I'd made. However, I finally came to the realization that I had done all I knew to do---and I could live with the results.

Stan was a mentor who mattered. *What?* His non-empathetic response may not have been just; however, it served me in future situations.

Stan taught me:

Always do your best. That brusque conversation with Stan taught me to always do your best. When you do your best, it makes is easier for you to live with the consequences. When you do your best, you don't live a life of regret.

This philosophy helped me when I was presented with the opportunity to be a sales columnist for the Denver Business Journal. Out of the blue, a colleague called me and shared that the DBJ had fired their current sales columnist and were looking for a replacement. I immediately called the editor and inquired about qualifications to be considered. He curtly informed me, "The deadline is tomorrow. Send me two original columns on sales by 8:00 am."

Small problem.

I wasn't a writer. Creating two original columns in less than twenty-four hours was the equivalent of running a marathon without training. What was I thinking?

Previous mentor learnings showed up. Jan Gruber whispered, "Show up and try. You might discover a talent you didn't know you had." Sister Emma made an appearance. "Where there is a will, there is a way. Go for it. Run the race, sing a new song, drive a different vehicle to success."

I stepped up to the challenge and wrote for eight hours, gulping down cups of coffee. I ignored the reappearing negative self-talk that told me, "Give it up, this is too hard." Instead, I reminded myself of the conversation with Stan. If I wasn't chosen as a columnist, I could live with that. I knew I couldn't live with the regret of not doing my best, not giving it my all. I wrapped up at 1:00 am in the morning. Two original columns sent. I had done my best.

About two weeks later, I received a call from Bruce Goldberg, one of the editors at the Denver Business Journal. "Congratulations, you've been selected as the new sales columnist." I thanked Bruce for the opportunity, hung up the phone and engaged in an all-out five-minute happy dance in my office. It was a great day.

It was the first step in me becoming a writer; a big step in building my brand.

A bad boss can also provide mentorship. Whenever I've been tempted to take a shortcut, I'm reminded of Stan's jab. "You didn't get the job done." Those words drive me to do everything in my power to do my best. Those words remind me to walk down the extra mile road. Then, and only then can I live with and accept the outcome, positive or negative. I've never desired to have a membership in the club, "If Only I Had."

I've learned to live with failure and the associated lessons. That's going to happen if you choose to show up and try new adventures.

Stan taught me how to live a no regrets life, one where you do your best with what you have. Sometimes a bad boss can also be a good boss.

Chapter 8
A Diamond in the Rough by Colleen

My sweaty palms gripped the steering wheel as I rehearsed my interview speech over and over, speeding down I–80 to the Omaha airport.

Six months earlier, my husband's boss, Jim, was in town for a managerial meeting. Brad's business as a Josten's sales representative was growing fast, so I'd been helping him sell class rings, awards, graduation announcements, caps, gowns, etc. Brad's boss was a sharp dresser with an equally sharp mind for sales and opportunities. Over coffee, he told us about a small company in Memphis, Tennessee, Varsity Spirit Corporation. "They're exploding and looking to build out a direct sales team. It would be a really good opportunity for the two of you because their customers are in the same schools as yours. And Colleen, because you were a cheerleader, this would be more in your court, as they are in the cheerleading and dance instruction and uniform business."

Hmmm. Jan Grubers words resounded. If I showed up and tried, I might discover a talent I didn't know I had, and it may be great.

I took Jim and Jan's advice. All summer, I called and called Varsity, but there was no return call. I left messages with various people because I had no clue who I should connect with. I imagined stacks of sticky notes with my name, number with an added notation… "She won't take no for an answer. Return her call!"

Finally, I connected and secured an interview. I rapidly repeated my pitch on my way to pick up Don Trandem, the Vice-President of Sales and Marketing for Varsity and Sherry Nymen, Director of Customer Service, at the airport. The obvious obstacles rattled in my brain. I did not have extensive experience in sales. I talked too much and listened too little, the kiss of death in sales. While I had been a cheerleader, I knew nothing about the cheerleading and dance uniform business.

However, I did know how to show up and try.

We went to a popular local restaurant for my interview. My excitement and nerves propelled me into a hyper stream of words, leaving little room for silence or listening. Finally, I gasped for a deep breath and, hoping to bolster my chances, said, "Excuse me while I go to my car and get my official résumé." As I re-entered the restaurant, I caught sight of Don and Sherry through the glass partition, their hands mimicking exaggerated chatter, flapping open and closed like talking puppets. My stomach sank. I had blown the interview.

Don looked at Sherry. Sherry looked at Don. With simultaneous nods, they said, "You're hired."

Thankfully, they had an innate ability to identify diamonds in the rough. They looked beyond my chattering like a chipmunk and instead focused on what the company needed: someone with a strong work ethic and passion for the company and their products. They looked beyond my unqualified resume and hired me to create a brand-new sales territory.

With a new briefcase in hand, I flew to the corporate office in Memphis for "fire hose" training and flew back home drowning in product knowledge. That's when the second phase of the training kicked in, the GGG program. Go Get 'um. Good luck!

There's good and bad news when joining a small, fast-growing company. The good news is they give people like me an opportunity. The bad news is they have limited time and resources for training and coaching because everyone is running fast and furious.

Lucky for me, Varsity had already recruited tenured salespeople from other companies who were well-versed in this industry.

Betty Black and Lanette White were such people. They were a couple of "tough old broads." Lanette could make a drag on a cigarette last longer than a minute. Betty could take you out with one look of an eye peering over her thick-rimmed glasses. However, beneath their tough exteriors were two hearts filled with generosity and empathy, especially for diamonds in the rough.

On more than one occasion, I frantically called for coaching on how to sell a new product or deal with an upset customer. (You have no idea how mad cheerleading moms get when Buffy's pom poms don't arrive on time!)

Betty generally answered, listening intently to my latest dilemma. Then she'd yell, "Lanette, pick up the phone! Our girl has got herself in trouble again! Now go ahead darlin',' tell us more about what is going on."

The conversations lasted ten, twenty, or thirty minutes.

These busy, successful salespeople always gave me the time. They didn't do it because they wanted recognition. No one at the corporate office knew I was bugging them. They weren't giving so they could receive. I was barely staying afloat, so I was unequipped to reciprocate with anything but a heartfelt thank you.

I suspect they did it because they knew if they could help get the "youngsters up and running," the diamonds in the rough polished, Varsity would become a big company, a great company. They were correct. Today, it is the largest company in the world in their industry.

Don, Sherry, Betty, and Lanette taught me:

Pay attention to diamonds in the rough. After starting my own business, an eager young woman, Annie, called me inquiring about our public enrollment sales training programs. "I'm with a small company, and they aren't willing to pay for any type of training. So, I'm going to pay for my own." (Hint: this is what future rock stars do.)

Annie enrolled in our sales training boot camp, and I discounted the enrollment fee. Sherry and Don gave me that first opportunity, and I wanted to do the same. Remembering the many generous and supportive conversations with Betty and Lanette, I gave her additional coaching sessions at no extra charge.

It takes a sales village... to win and retain business. I've shared this message, evolved from my experience with Betty and Lanette, with hundreds of sales teams. It's important for busy, seasoned professionals to pay attention to the diamonds in the rough crossing their paths. Slow down to offer time and advice to polish those potential diamonds. One person cannot scale a company. However, people helping people will build a successful village.

Chapter 9
It's Not Just A Numbers Game by Colleen

It was the best of times and the worst of times. Through hard work and mentorship, in four years I had built a great sales territory for Varsity, from the ground up. I was now the dominant player in my market.

And Brad and I were filing for divorce. This was not on my "goal board." As with any major loss, I experienced a floodgate of emotions: heartbreaking sadness, discouragement at failing, embarrassment, anger... and a severe reality check.

The reality was that I didn't want to stay in Omaha. Brad and I had been a toned-down version of Barbie and Ken. Ken was moving to Minneapolis for a promotion. Barbie wasn't sure of her next move. Do I stay? Try something new? Lifeguard in the Bahamas?

I scheduled a meeting with my boss and swallowed past the lump in my throat. "Don, I just don't want to keep calling on the same schools Brad and I had." Don was sympathetic and listened intently. Then I added the big request, "I'd like to be a regional sales manager."

There were a few minor challenges to my request. First, there was no such position currently available. Varsity was still in lean, building mode. I'd have to bring new ideas and plans to justify creating a new position. This led to the second challenge: I had no sales management experience. (Do you see a common theme?)

Incredibly, Don took another chance on me. "Let's give it a shot."

I flew to Memphis to meet with Varsity CEO, Jeff Webb, to interview for a job that didn't exist. Prior to the meeting, Don coached me on how to present the business case for creating this role. He encouraged me to share my entrepreneurial spirit and how it would help Varsity make more money and gain market share. Besides working as an independent contractor for Varsity, I was also running a side business selling products Varsity didn't carry such as tennis shoes, camp wear, letter jackets, to name a few. This combination of chaos and creativity meant I worked evenings and weekends, billing, packing, and shipping goods.

The big interview began. Don said, "Go ahead. Tell Jeff how many tennis shoes you sold under your other company last year." I wasn't sure if my answer would get me hired or fired; however, I hoped the truth would set me free.

"Over 500 pair," I answered.

Jeff's eyebrows raised so I got braver. "And if Varsity adds tennis shoes to our catalog, I can sell a lot more."

Don's smile widened because he'd been campaigning to carry this product line. Jeff's eyebrows lowered and I continued to share other products I was selling "on the side." I flew home and waited for the telephone to ring. A few weeks later I received the call, "You are now the Regional Sales Manager of the Midwest and will be in charge of ten states. My heart skipped a beat with joy… and trepidation.

Don's mentorship didn't stop there, as he demonstrated great kindness during that next year. Anyone who has gone through the loss of a spouse, partner, child or friend knows the first year is full of many difficult firsts. The first birthday celebration without this person. The first anniversary alone. The first new holiday tradition without him or her.

For me, the first Christmas loomed. And I dreaded it. How could Barbie go home without Ken? How could I answer the question, "Why didn't it work out?"

Out of the blue, Don asked, "Would you be open to coming back early from your vacation to help me put together the sales budget?" Before he could finish his sentence, I answered, "Yes!"

Now, let me be clear. Don didn't need help with the sales budget. He was a whiz with numbers and had a background in finance and banking. I suspect he sensed my angst and stepped in to bolster me through a difficult first. *It was a mentor moment.*

This wasn't in his job description of a Vice President of Sales. His job was to bring in the sales numbers. However, wise people recognize that if you take care of your people, they will take care of the numbers.

But the help didn't stop with Don.

In my newly minted role, I sat in my new office with a window, a big desk, and a door with my name on it. It's hard to describe my feelings as I held my new business cards: Regional Sales Manager. The word terrified comes to mind. I was afraid my new bosses, the ones who had put their trust in me, would discover I was in way over my head. *Just what does a Regional Sales Manager do? Where is the handbook?* There weren't any YouTube videos to watch or podcasts to listen to.

I made calls to my sales team, lined up dates to travel with them and analyzed sales numbers. I was busy; however, I knew I wasn't being that productive.

My inner voice was getting quite loud. *Why did you ask for this job? Who do you think you are? You're just a small-town kid from Iowa.* The loudest voice shouted, *they are going to find out you're in over your head. When is the pink slip conversation going to happen?*

About three months into my new position, the General Manager, Kline Boyd, stopped by my office. Kline is a southern gentleman, a kind person AND was one of the original investors in the company. He had a lot riding on the success of any new hire. I braced myself for the pink slip conversation.

"Got a minute?"

I thought, *Sure, getting fired should only take a minute.*

"Colleen, I have been observing you, and you are putting up a really good front."

I gulped. *Here it comes.*

"However, I know you're struggling because of your personal situation and this new position. So, I just came in to remind you that if you ever need someone to talk to, my office is right down the hall, and I would welcome that conversation." He got up to leave and turned around. "And Colleen, one more thing. You're going to be just fine. You've got what it takes to do this job. Teach your team what you know."

My eyes teared, and I fought back an ugly cry at this unexpected show of empathy. My inner conversations changed. *If this savvy businessman thinks I can make it, maybe, just maybe, I can.*

My confidence increased; my anxiety decreased. I realized that I knew more than I thought I did. My job was to teach everything I had learned in building a territory from the ground up. I could do that! Two years later, my region was the number one region in the country.

It would be easy to take credit for my competence to lead and manage a team, but the credit goes to two mentors who took believed in and encouraged me. They instilled confidence in me that I had what it takes and "everything is going to be just fine."

Don and Kline taught me:

Pay attention. I didn't share my worries or self-doubt with Don or Kline. However, great leaders pay attention to the verbal and non-verbal communication cues. They tune into the emotional state of another human being, giving them the gifts of empathy and compassion. In sales, we talk a lot about revenue, bonuses or commission. As a grateful recipient of their empathy, I've taught these skills to thousands of clients. It's better than any bonus check.

Look for the potential in others, beyond the resume. Dig deeper to learn about a person's passion, values, and work ethic. Don and Kline influenced me in making a great hire for my Business Development Manager.

Julie Points' resume didn't match the position requirements since her most recent position was warehouse manager. She had no sales experience. However, I knew the role of a warehouse manager was not easy because of my background in distribution and manufacturing.

Because Don and Kline taught me to look beyond the resume, I scheduled the first interview. I'll never forget the question---and answer---that sealed the deal. "Tell me about a time when you had to teach yourself a new skill with little guidance or resources." Julie's response still makes me laugh.

"One of my jobs right out of high school was working for an event company that supplied all the stuff for birthday parties, including clowns. At the eleventh hour before a party, the assigned clown called in sick. I wasn't going to let a bunch of little kids down, so I bought a kit with instruction manual, taught myself how to make animal balloons, donned the clown outfit, and made the day for the birthday girl."

That's called initiative. That's problem-solving. That was my next hire. Julie and I have worked together for over ten years. She has demonstrated the values we all want in a good team member: Dedication, hard work and the ability to learn and adapt. She's mastered skills in social media, editing videos, editing books, running events… the list goes on. I'm blessed to have this wing woman by my side, all because I was taught to look beyond the resume.

Chapter 10
It Only Takes One Conversation by Colleen

Dozens of excited teenage girls and boys milled around, giggling, dancing, and chatting. At 9:00 p.m., I sat in a studio at our annual catalog shoot, where the film crew photographed the latest fashions in cheer and dancewear. Our designer Craig Tallman was "fussing" over every piece of hair and clothing to make sure the photos were perfect. And they were.

My head nodded in fatigue, not just because of the time of day but because Don Trandem, my boss and mentor, had given his notice. During the exhaustive search for a new VP of Sales and Marketing, some of his responsibilities landed on my desk, because I was the only Regional Sales Manager in the corporate office. I had sixteen direct reports on my sales team, and the long days were catching up even with my blessing of abundant energy.

Jeff Webb, the CEO of Varsity, quietly took a seat next to me, engaging in small talk. Then, small talk quickly turned into big talk when he posed the question, "Why aren't you applying for Don's job as VP of Sales?"

I stammered out my excuses. "I've only been in my role as a Regional Sales Manager for two years. I really like the team I am managing. I'm considering moving out of the corporate office to become a field sales manager, like my counterparts."

Jeff listened attentively but didn't buy my excuses. He kept gently pressing with more questions about why I wasn't applying for the job.

As cheerleaders and dancers passed by us modeling the latest fashions, I finally fessed up. "I'm not ready."

Jeff's answer was not what I expected. "We know. We'll help you get ready."

It was a mentor moment.

Huh...if this smart businessman thinks I can do this job, maybe, just maybe I can.

A few days later, I said yes, and I ended right back where I've been so many times ...in over my head.

Like a human dog paddling across the Pacific Ocean.

Climbing a fifty-foot ladder, one where you can't even see the next rung, that was me... again.

But true to Jeff's promise, help showed up. Our Chief Financial Officer, Bob Dunseath, reached down and pulled me up to the next rung. One of my new responsibilities included setting and managing a sales budget. It was a much more comprehensive and complicated than the budget I had as a regional sales manager

We were all crazy busy during regular working hours, so on more than one occasion, Bob stayed late after work to help me learn the ins and outs of budgeting. He smiled patiently as I worked to understand the key performance metrics of a profit and loss statement. "Can you explain one more time how to..."

Like Betty and Lanette, Bob didn't receive recognition or compensation for the overtime hours. He could have easily taken the attitude, "Well, you folks promoted her. You deal with her lack of skills. I'm not her boss."

Some of the most successful organizations are filled with wise, caring mentors like Bob, who give more than expected in their roles and responsibilities. They spot diamonds in the rough, who, with a little polishing and education, can become a real asset to the organization's growth and mission.

Eventually, I led a team of 130 salespeople. Because of the tutelage and care provided by others, I became proficient at leading a team, creating accurate sales targets and territories, which continued to fuel growth.

Jeff and Bob taught me:

Believe in people. A few years ago, a young woman, Brook, set an appointment with me. She was an executive assistant for a property and casualty insurance company. I immediately knew she was sharp because of how she'd prepared for our meeting. She posed thoughtful questions, welcomed feedback, and her desire to succeed oozed out of her every pore. She had approached her bosses on multiple occasions about her desire to get into sales, only to hear, "Well, let's talk about it in a few months." She told me, "I know I can be successful in sales; I just need a chance, and I'm willing to invest in gaining skills to get the opportunity."

As I listened, I heard Jeff's words, "We'll help get you ready."

I replied, "I'm here to help. We'll get you ready."

She enrolled in our public sales training course, and like Annie, this diamond in the rough also received extra coaching at no charge. No pats on the back for me but for the mentors who modeled generosity to me.

Brook quit her job, applied at another firm for a role in sales, and, as the old saying goes, the rest is history. She became a top producer, and this diamond in the rough is shining brightly.

Be patient. Whenever I feel impatient, I roll back in time and remember the patience shown to me when I was new and naïve. It helps me to "get over myself" because the memories quickly temper my hard driving, results oriented behavior as I recall the grace given to me when learning new knowledge and skills.

Chapter 11
The Golden Rule by Colleen

In my second year as VP of Sales, life was good. All our hard work was paying off; the sales team and sales were expanding. Growing up on a farm, I learned the value and expectations of hard work. My family worked six days a week, taking Sunday off for church and rest. So, imagine my surprise when I learned my overachieving work ethic was not always the key to success.

I marched down the hall for my annual performance review with Kline. (You remember him from the kind conversation in Chapter Six.) With a slight air of arrogance, I prepared myself to hear accolades and thanks in this easy-peasy review. Sales were up, and we were becoming the Goliath in the industry.

The performance review conversation began with such and then the conversation took a right turn. "Colleen, I want you to know how much I appreciate your work ethic. You're first in and last out. None of us doubt your dedication to this company or your team." I beamed with pride. "However, some things need to change."

What? My heart pumped harder. My smile slowly disappeared, as did my "easy-peasy" performance review.

"You come into this office, so focused on your job, that you no longer look left or right. I've seen times when you don't even say hi to your assistant, who is often here as early as you. That has to change."

I don't remember anything else about the conversation, as emotions clouded my thinking. Robotically, I slowly walked back to my desk with tangled emotions and thoughts: Anger. *I am giving my all to this company. Who is he to criticize when I'm getting a ton of work done?* Sarcasm. *What am I supposed to do? Hold a tea party in my office at 3:00 pm?* Confusion. *What is he talking about?*

Then, my self-awareness and humility muscles kicked in.

Kline was right. *I'm not paying attention to the very people helping me in my role. I'm a nice person. (Wasn't I elected homecoming queen?)* Ugh. *When did I become a person who got so focused on the goal that I lost focus on the most essential things in life: relationships with the people with whom I live and work?*

Kline lived by the Golden Rule and expected others to do the same... treat others the way you want to be treated. It didn't matter if you were the IT genius in the building. It didn't matter if you achieved sales goals and brought revenue into the company. What mattered to him most was your treatment of people.

What a lesson and gift to me at such an early age.

Today, this type of conversation is called a crucial conversation, a CAREfrontaton conversation. Kline cared enough to have what could have been a contentious discussion. He cared enough to point out my blind spots impacting me and others.

Because of that conversation, I changed.

I finally lifted my head up and looked around instead of down to add more things to my to-do list. I greeted my assistant with a smile and increased appreciation. "Thanks a million for everything." Something as simple as going to the break room and restroom changed. I acknowledged those I passed with a simple smile or "How's your day going?" Instead of being deep in thought as I hustled past the customer service team, I said, "Thanks for all your help. My team so appreciates you," or "How is your day going?"

Just like I wanted to be treated.

Kline taught me:

Hold CAREfrontation conversations. Leaders in their homes, businesses, and communities must have the courage to confront bad behavior, regardless of a person's title, contribution, or stature.

In my current role as a consultant and teacher, I've had to hold a few of these conversations. I was coaching a CEO struggling with a very talented executive on her team who consistently violated the Golden Rule. After several coaching conversations, this employee was unwilling to change and continued to poison the company culture with his lack of respect for others.

Posters of the company values were hanging on the CEO's wall and in office hallways. I shared, "Based on what you are tolerating from him, perhaps you need to purchase new posters, ones that read: We value respect and teamwork unless you bring in a lot of money. In that case we tolerate all jerks and lack of respect."

She looked at me stunned, then smiled, then frowned again. "Of course, I need to fire him." To her surprise, employee after employee came into her office, thanking her for getting rid of a toxic individual. The team stepped up to fill the void until a replacement was found. Her culture changed, and her business grew.

Get back on track with The Golden Rule. When I started my own company, I hired a consultant, who was experiencing the trifecta of life difficulties... a rebellious teenage daughter creating many sleepless nights; a sad, unexpected divorce; a beloved aging, ailing mother growing weaker by the day.

I'd like to say that I demonstrated the Golden Rule right away. I did not. Once again, my task-driven, goal-oriented behavior ran full throttle. I didn't offer enough empathy or support because we had a goal to hit!

After one particularly non-empathetic conversation, it struck me: You're not honoring the Golden Rule. I'd regressed. Ugh. There I was again, looking down instead of up and around. There was dissonance in who I said I was and my actual behavior. Double ugh.

I scheduled a meeting with her with only one goal: to say, "I'm sorry. Please forgive me." That difficult conversation still makes me wonder, who was that person who got so far off track?

The good news is we are still good friends. I credit her for the ability to forgive and Kline for being the mentor who reinforced the Golden Rule. I'm a work in progress as that task-oriented, hit-the-goal-and-leave-bloodied-bodies-on-the-way-up personality sometimes pokes its rascal head up. But the performance review from years ago, centered around living and modeling the Golden Rule, continues to keep me in check.

Chapter 12
A New Season by Colleen

"What am I thinking? This is a great job with a great company. What if I fall flat on my face?" Varsity was growing, and a recognized leader in the school spirit industry, yet this nagging feeling to pursue my dream of being a full-time speaker and trainer wouldn't leave my mind. I recalled a phrase from Ecclesiastes, "For there is a season and a time for every matter under heaven." I felt my season as vice president of sales coming to an end.

Jan Grubers voice nudged me again. "Show up and try. Sometimes, you'll discover a talent you didn't know you had. And sometimes you will become great."

I gave five months' notice and crossed my fingers, hoping I wouldn't regret this decision. Varsity graciously accepted my resignation and fully supported my career move into training, speaking, and coaching. On the final evening of the national sales meeting, my final responsibility, they surprised me with a Rolex watch. I choked back tears and blurted, "I better not lose this." I admitted to the colleague beside me, "The nicest watch I've ever owned was a rubber running watch." What a great send-off.

John Denver's, "Rocky Mountain High" song was playing in my head as I drove to Colorado. However, this was not a well-thought-out move. I had no big business plan, just big goals and ambitions. It's good that angels work overtime because I didn't know anyone in

Denver, and I had no network to tap into for advice, leads, or support. But I sure loved the mountains! With no idea how to enter this sales training and speaking field, I was simply showing up. *Have I taken Jan's advice a little too far?*

Finding a place to live posed problems. Oddly, people are reluctant to rent to someone without a job. Fortunately, I learned of a Sandler Sales Training franchise. Driving to my first interview, I got lost and headed to the airport instead of their office. Thankfully, the franchise owners didn't hold my tardiness against me and, after several interviews, hired me as an associate. Things were looking up. "I'm on my way to a great speaking and training career!"

But it was hard. I worked on straight commission and had no sales leads handed to me. Once again, I was building a sales pipeline from the ground up. I spent long hours cold calling, giving free marketing talks, and attending association lunches serving up bad chicken dishes. I attended disappointing networking events where the majority showed up with one goal. "Let me tell you about me and my business." Then, "Let me tell you a bit more about me."

Despite all this prospecting activity, I heard more no's than yes's. Self-doubt set in… again. *Should I have stayed with Varsity? What was I thinking moving to a city where I had no connections?*

Three months into my new venture, I called Lynette Wieger, a good friend of twenty years. She took over my Omaha territory at Varsity when I moved to Memphis. She knew me well and was familiar with both my strengths and weaknesses. I shared my worries. "Do I have the chops to make it in this business? Maybe this speaking career is just too big of a leap. Should I find a safe corporate job with a salary and 401K?" I closed my eyes and crossed my fingers, secretly hoping she'd agree. Surely, she'd encourage me to take a more financially stable job.

Lynette took a breath and paused. "Well, you certainly didn't choose the easiest next step on your career path. I've known you for twenty years, and you've accomplished hard things before. If anyone can do it, you can."

I uncrossed my fingers and took the conversation as a sign to move on.

One hot summer day, standing in our office parking lot, I shared my anxiety about my continued lack of sales and money with Gary Harvey, the Sandler Franchise owner. He listened intently and said, "The first year is the most difficult. It's not easy for anyone. You've got what it takes to make it in this business. Don't ever forget that."

"Thanks, Gary." The right words at the right time.

Later, at Sandler conference, John Rosso, a very successful franchisee, struck up a conversation with me. A master at tuning into the emotional temperature of other people, he noted my anxiety. "Colleen, let's change your goals. Instead of being so focused on getting a yes from prospects, I want you to set a goal to get one hundred no's as fast as you can."

I muttered, "The good news is I'm well on my way to achieving that goal!"

He explained, "By the time you get one hundred no's, you will have heard every objection, question, and provocative statement derailing you on a call. Learn a lesson from each of those no's, and I promise you that you'll be well on your way to one hundred yes's."

Hmmm. It never occurred to me that a no, a negative, could be a positive. My anxiety cloud lifted. I conducted more effective appointments because I wasn't worried about prospects saying no. I focused on my new goal of learning a lesson. "Great! Another no!"

And lo and behold, because I wasn't showing up anxious and needy, I started closing more business. Today, I recognize that John deployed a psychological principle called reframing. He helped me look at a negative, a no, in a positive way. That one conversation was a defining one for me.

Another franchisee also provided time and wisdom. Bill Bartlett ran a big sales training business. Rumor was he commanded one thousand dollars an hour for his coaching services. At a Sandler conference, he offered to take me to lunch. I was surprised and flattered that a big dog wanted to invest time with a little dog.

Wanting to impress him, I initially acted like everything was just great. He saw through my façade and asked, "What isn't going great? He seemed sincere, so I blurted, "Well, the owner of a large, well-known wealth management company recently hired me to conduct a series of workshops. After the second one, he asked me into his big office and told me the content didn't meet his expectations. He fired me on the spot! And then, turned around and began typing on his computer! I didn't know what to do. Was I supposed to let myself out? Say thanks for your time. It was awful."

Bill nodded. "Colleen, here's what happened. Your client was sitting in the BIG chair, and he made sure you were sitting in the SMALL chair. He wanted to make you feel little and diminished. Don't let anyone ever do that to you again. Everyone deserves to be treated with respect and dignity."

Armored with that advice and desire to continually improve, I found the courage to follow-up with other participants in the workshop to learn what I could have done better. All responded the same. "We loved the training."

Finally, one participant lowered her voice and hesitantly shared the real scoop behind my firing. "Colleen, your content focused on not letting your self-worth be defined by titles and trappings. That's exactly what the owner of this company is all about. His self-worth is based on how large his house is, the type of car he drives, and the clothes he wears. It's no wonder he fired you. You exposed his true-life philosophy."

But the story doesn't end there.

One morning, my wonderful new husband, Jim Stanley, sat sipping his coffee and reading the paper. "Hey, remember that guy who fired you? Well, he's sentenced to one hundred years in prison for embezzling millions from his clients."

You can't make this stuff up.

Lynette, Gary, John, and Bill taught me:

Never miss a moment to encourage. Often, people don't need more knowledge or skill training. They need to hear, "You've got this. You are capable of this. Yes, it's hard, but you've done hard stuff before."

After one of my keynotes, a young lady walked up and said, "Thank you. I appreciated you sharing stories of how the tough times precede the hard times. Speakers like you look perfect, so it is nice to hear the backstory of what it really takes to be successful. It was just what I needed to hear today." I was happy to have provided a mentor moment.

Reframe negatives into a positive. I have shared my "go for the no" story with thousands of people and clients. It's always rewarding to watch the light bulbs appear over their heads as they discover the power of achieving a positive from a negative.

I ask clients, "What lessons did you learn from the no's in your life?"

- "I'm a more compassionate person because of this adversity."
- "I learned a valuable lesson sooner rather than later in life."
- "If I can handle this, I can tackle anything."
- "It's made me grateful for things I've taken for granted."
- "I'm more willing to take risks and avoid the no progress, comfort zone."
- "This lesson has made me smarter for my next meeting."

Expect and demand respect. It's essential to receive difficult feedback. Without it, we aren't capable of seeing our blind spots. It's okay to disagree with one another. What's not okay is disrespectful words and actions. We can disagree without being disagreeable. Bill's insights served me well, particularly when meeting with potential clients. I have disqualified multiple opportunities, not because they can't use my services but because they tried to put me in a SMALL chair. This mindset allows me to work with good people where the client and I sit in equally BIG chairs.

Chapter 13
The Kick Butt Program by Colleen

After two and half years working as a Sandler associate, I felt stuck. At that time, there wasn't a place for an associate to advance in the organization.

So once again, I showed up, tried and started my own business, SalesLeadership, which I still run today. Entrepreneurship is not easy. You spend long hours as the CEO, marketing director, operations manager and head dishwasher. While I knew this was the right move, I missed the mentor moments and camaraderie with my Sandler colleagues.

Divine intervention made another appearance and a new mentor in Jill Konrath, a friendly, smart, hardy Minnesotan, showed up. Always blazing new trails, she was one of the first female sales reps hired by Xerox back in the 1970s. From there she started her own sales consultancy and authored four bestselling sales books.

When we met at a National Speakers Association conference, she was the leading woman in the sales training industry with over 300,000 raving fans subscribing to her newsletters. We hit it off immediately, exchanging Ole and Lena jokes understood only by Minnesotans. I was thrilled when Jill invited me to speak at her sales conference for women in sales in Minneapolis. This dramatically changed the trajectory of my career.

After that conference, Jill decided the speakers needed to stay connected, and she formed a mastermind group of sales speakers and trainers. *It was my group of Vagabonds.* I showed up to the first meeting in Minneapolis with ten or eleven women, all running some type of sales consultancy. These alpha females with big personalities and big opinions offered challenging questions and amazing support.

Initially, I was a little tentative. After all, did I really want to share my "trade secrets" with competitors? Looking back, I realize I was coming from a place of scarcity, not abundance.

Thank goodness, Jill had enough abundance for all of us. She viewed us as mustard seeds. This parable from the bible teaches that something seemingly small and insignificant can grow to be quite significant.

Many of us in that mastermind group ran small businesses. We were really good at our crafts; however, Jill was emphatic, "Not enough people know about your good work." She encouraged us "mustard seeds" to author books. She used her reputation and influence to introduce fledgling authors like me to AMACOM, a publishing house later purchased by Harper Collins. I landed a book contract, without an agent, because of Jill.

Upon the launch of my book, Emotional Intelligence For Sales Success, Jill's generosity continued. She wrote the forward to the book and then promoted it to her 300,000 newsletter subscribers. In the world of sales, this is the equivalent of landing on Oprah's book club! My book showed up on the first page of Google searches. Sales professionals paid attention, and it has been translated into eight languages. Speaking engagements followed in Warsaw, Venice, Vienna, Milan and Bismark, North Dakota followed. It caught the attention of the mega company Salesforce, and they named me as one of the top seven most influential sales figures of the twenty-first century. (Please note my family still wonders what I do for a living.)

It would be easy to say Jill did this because she had a lot of time on her hands. Not true. She was a busy mom with two children. Her husband was fighting a long-term battle with liver disease.

Jill is like so many great mentors; generously taking the time when they don't have time to help others, sowing seeds of encouragement to help people reach their full potential.

Jill taught me:

Share the spotlight. Instead of being the top dog woman in sales training, hogging the spotlight, Jill pulled others up and along because of her innate spirt of generosity. Many of us mentees proudly say we are graduates of the Jill Konrath kick-butt program with boot marks on our pants to prove it.

Collaborate rather than compete. Create your Vagabond group. After Jill stepped down, Lori Richardson led the mastermind group for ten years. Now, it's a non-profit, Women's Sales Experts, run by volunteer members embracing the spirit of generosity and collaboration planted by Jill so many years ago.

We promote each other's work because we've learned there is room for all of us. Friends now, we meet once a year in person, hold quarterly learning sessions, and reach out regularly to one another with questions or challenges. We work hard to hit our sales quota and equally hard to hit the fun quota. I've laughed until my sides hurt. There is nothing like getting a group of alpha women in the room to stir up magical conversations.

Be a mustard seed. Besides business mentoring, I believe in supporting non-profit organizations with time, talent and money. Since teaching is my talent, I offer my services free of charge to select non-profits, to be a mustard seed, helping others reach their potential, especially those from difficult backgrounds.

Chapter 14
A Full Circle Moment by Colleen

"Colleen, Bill Seely...am I catching you at an okay time?" Bill and I worked together in our thirties at Varsity Spirit Corporation. He was on the cheerleading instruction side of the business, and I was on the uniform side of the business. Today, Bill is the president of Varsity Spirit Corporation.

"Always good to hear from you Bill. What's going on?" Secretly, I was hoping he was calling to invite me back to speak at one of their sales meetings.

"Colleen, congratulations. I'm calling to let you know that you've been selected as a Varsity Legend."

My mind raced. I had heard of this select group. To date, it's sixty-five individuals chosen from over hundreds of employees who have worked or currently work at Varsity. It's awarded because of the impact made to create the cheerleading and dance phenomenon that we see in America today.

I gulped, held back tears of surprise and joy and managed to say, "Wow, this is great. Thank you." Walking into my home that evening, I greeted my husband with a huge smile. "Honey, you are looking at a legend."

A few months later, I flew to Carlsbad, California, for the Varsity Spirit National Sales Rally, where new legends are honored. As the plane descended, my mind filled with memories. The mentorship I had received. The crazy and wonderful sales meetings. The frustration of learning how to sell and lead. The long hours worked at a fast growth company. Incentive trips to France and Austria. The countless lessons learned.

When it was time to accept the award at the recognition ceremony, I stepped up to the microphone and took a breath.

"I come here today with one word: gratitude. I'm grateful for the many opportunities Varsity gave me. I was a wildcard—no sales experience, just a whole lot of passion and a work ethic that wouldn't quit." I shared stories of the mentors who shaped me, of the leaders who challenged me, and the teammates who walked alongside me.

And I ended with this:

"I wouldn't be here today—doing what I'm doing, teaching what I'm teaching—without the years I spent at Varsity."

It was a full circle moment. A moment where the mentee got to say thank you. To acknowledge the many people who saw something in me before I saw it in myself.

And to recognize that none of us gets here on our own.

Chapter 15
Two-and-a-half Cents by LeAnn

All 200 students from kindergarten through twelfth grade crowded into the school gymnasium. We first graders sat near the free-throw line, facing the stage at the end of the gym. The giggling, squiggling, and elbowing ceased when we heard the click of the movie projector, and the reel began showing the film. Danny Kaye, a popular actor, singer, and dancer during that time in the 1950s, sat on an overturned barrel interacting with starving children as he toured in support of UNICEF, United Nations International Children's Relief Fund. I sat enthralled as I watched children of all shapes, colors, and sizes clamor around him, eager for his attention and nutritious treats.

At the supper table that night, my seven brothers and sisters and I told Mom and Dad what we'd seen and learned. "Two-and-a-half cents can buy a carton of milk and save a little kid's life!" I exclaimed as I drank mine.

Mary piped up. "And this year, we can trick-or-treat-for UNICEF."

So, we four girls donned our homemade costumes. This ghost couldn't see through the holes in the sheet, so my sisters helped lead me through the streets of our little rural town, collecting money for needy children all over the world. "Trick-or-treat for UNICEF!" we chirped over and over. "Every penny helps!"

The next month, I sat in church staring at the poster hanging from the podium, portraying a starving child with a big, bloated belly and sad eyes filled with tears. "We're having a Thanksgiving clothing drive," Father Scallon said. "Bring any good used clothing to send to the poor." As I squirmed in the pew, Danny Kaye's film played over and over in my mind.

So, my brothers, sisters, and I went home and tried on all our hand-me-down clothes. If it didn't fit Bob, Denny, Diane, Mary, Theresa or Keith, I tried it on since I was the runt of the litter. If it didn't fit me, we boxed it up for the clothing drive. In retrospect, I think we were relatively poor Iowa farm folk at the time, but I felt rich that day.

Danny Kaye was an influencer who made a lifelong impact on me and the rest of the world long before Instagram, TikTok, or Facebook.

Danny Kaye taught me:

Share the "wealth." When Mark and I raised our trio, we coached them to give a portion of their meager allowances to a children's relief fund. Every few months, we received a photo and letter from Musa, a young boy in Africa, telling us how their money had helped. "We bought seven bags of grain," he wrote with gratitude and enthusiasm as if they were bags of gold. Today, our kids have generous hearts and wallets.

Every penny counts. Too often, we believe our small contributions aren't worth donating; they can't make much difference. Yet, consider there are 335 million people in the United States. If everyone donated one cent, that would be 3,350,000 dollars. If everyone donated a dollar, 335 million dollars would go a long way to help people in need. Consider putting loose change in every red kettle at Christmastime. And one dollar in each collection basket at church.

Tithe. As a Chicken Soup for the Soul author, I've read hundreds of stories of people who donated their last dollar to a charity and mysteriously got that and more back. Committing a small percentage of your income to a cause pays off for them and for you. I remember my mama writing checks for five dollars to support an Indian reservation in South Dakota. We didn't have much, but, as Daddy said, "I give to

God, and He gives back; it's just that His shovel is bigger than mine." Dad became a successful, generous farmer. The more you give, the more you receive. Try it.

Chapter 16
A Bountiful Harvest by LeAnn

Dad sat at the head of the table with my seven siblings and Mom. He and my brothers had just come in from spring planting and plowing. The stern look on his face told us he had a rare but poignant message and teaching moment to share.

To support eight children, Dad had a side business applying liquid fertilizer to our crops, our neighbor's, and other farmers crops. He had recently learned that another local farmer had started the exact business in competition with Dad. I had overheard some quiet conversations between him and Mom about the strain this would put on the friendship and our family's budget. This new competitor and his family had been to our home numerous times. While the grownups visited, their little girls, my sisters, and I spent many evenings catching fireflies, swinging on our homemade swing set, and playing softball in the yard until dark. I wondered if these little friends would still be my friends.

It seemed our frequent family prayers for rain and bountiful harvests had been unanswered for the past few years. And while Daddy said he would never let his stomach know he was poor; I sensed that dollars were tight. If the crops weren't good and the harvest was bad, would Daddy argue with this man now because we needed more money?

As Dad buttered one of Mama's homemade biscuits, we all waited for what we anticipated would be an important lesson, although Dad, a typical staunch German, was a man of few words. This one was his usual one sentence. "Never let a dollar come between friends."

I was too young to understand farm markets and crop reports after that. But I do remember catching fireflies and playing ball with my little friends... and that we got rain and many bountiful harvests.

Dad taught me:

Never let a dollar come between friends. When I wrote my first Chicken Soup for the Soul book, I was invited to coauthor it with a person on staff who became a dear friend. This wonderful woman's obligations, priorities, and life challenges prevented her from contributing a fair share of the work. So, it fell to me to read the 1,000 stories submitted. I had taken hundreds of hours of writing classes, mentoring, and studying to learn how to write a true personal story to write my first book. So, it fell to me to help select and rewrite the submissions "Chicken Soup style" for publication. Family, friends, and fellow writers often criticized, "It's not fair you are doing all the work." Sometimes I agreed, but I recalled what Daddy taught. And that book hit number seventeen on the New York Times Best Seller list... a bountiful harvest.

Chapter 17
It's Time for Supper by LeAnn

My brother was a victim of the Vietnam War.

Not only did he lose his right arm there, but years later, his peace, his joy, his life. In his numerous, ongoing attempts to heal his mind and soul, he sought counseling from someone I believe was a misguided, incompetent therapist. This man instructed Denny to meet with our mother in her home and angrily berate her for all the mistakes she had made raising him. A few weeks later, Mama wadded a handkerchief in her hands and wiped tears as she recounted to me the three hours of his painful, heart-wrenching criticism. As we cried together, my voice choked. "What did you do then, Mom?"

She swallowed back tears. "I took him supper."

Denny suffered for years with tortuous memories from that horrific war, resulting in devastating physical and mental health issues. For several heartbreaking years, he refused to engage in family gatherings, weddings, or communications. Throughout this time, Mom delivered love notes, lunches, and suppers, often leaving them on his doorstep a few miles from hers. By the grace of God, years later, Denny healed. And danced with us at wedding celebrations!

As Mama lay in hospice, preparing for her transition into heaven, he stood at her side multiple times throughout the days and tiptoed in the dark quiet of the nights. Today, Denny and Mom are dancing together in heaven.

Mama taught me and everyone who knew her:

Demonstrate love unconditionally. It's often easy to repeat words of love, but there's a difference between saying them and putting them into action. There was nothing that anyone, friend or family member, could ever do for which Mom would withhold her demonstration of love. Today, when people I care about struggle with family relationship issues, I summarize my requested advice in one sentence. "Love and demonstrate that love unconditionally. Never stop." This is, of course, much easier said than done. It's hard to offer love without expecting it to be returned, to detach ourselves from that hope or outcome. But it's worth it. Love always wins.

Chapter 18
Light a Single Candle by LeAnn

"It's better to light a single candle than to curse the darkness," I repeated over and over in my mind as I propped bottles for babies in cardboard box bassinets in a C–141 cargo jet. That slogan had hung over the doorway of a clinic in Vietnam where an American plastic surgeon established a facility to help the children burned and disfigured by the war.

As a volunteer for Friends of Children of Vietnam, I had agreed to fly to Vietnam in April 1975 to escort six babies back to their preassigned adoptive homes. As the plane circled Saigon, I peered out the window to see the runway lined with camouflaged fighter jets. I was in a war zone. After descending the 747's stairs, I walked across the sunbaked tarmac and into the arms of the overseas director of FCVN. She hugged me and exclaimed, "Have you heard the news? Last night, President Gerald Ford okayed Operation Babylift. You won't help us take out six babies but 300!"

So, five days later, I sat cross-legged in the belly of a massive cargo jet next to a row of twenty-two cardboard boxes, each containing three or four bawling babies. We nine volunteers discovered we could feed all one hundred babies by placing them each on their side and propping their bottles on the shoulder of their box mate. Some sucked formula down in only minutes, while others needed help. I cradled a baby girl on my folded legs and coaxed her to drink while using my left hand to feed another baby in the box. As bottles emptied, we draped diapers over our shoulders to burp one baby while propping another's bottle. Soon, the aircraft smelled of diarrhea and spit up, but we sweaty, disheveled volunteers smiled and even laughed. It was joyful work bringing these babies to freedom and families. When exhausted, I recalled the works and words of that heroic plastic surgeon as I fed our squalling cargo. "I'm lighting a single candle."

Our travels took the infants home via Clark Air Force Base in the Philippines to Hawaii, then Presidio in California, then Denver, Colorado, and finally to their adoptive mommies, daddies, brothers, and sisters all over the United States. Volunteers flew back to bring 200 more children before Vietnam fell to the Communists. Six other organizations scurried to do the same. As I cuddled babies on this unbelievable journey, I wept for all the children left behind ... the 50,000 Amerasian... half-American, half-Asian... orphans barely surviving there at the end of that war.

Three weeks after I returned home, on April 30th, 1975, Saigon fell to the Communists. Operation Babylift saved over three thousand children.

That heroic plastic surgeon taught me:

No effort is too small: Often, when we look at the massive injustices and suffering in the world, we're inclined to believe our small attempts would be insignificant. Yet every effort, no matter how small, makes a difference. Collectively, those differences cause changes, at least for individuals, if not eventually the whole country or the world. I became a part of Operation Babylift because three years previously, I had stopped to buy a dozen cupcakes at a bake sale supporting Friends of Children of Vietnam. Soon after I joined, I became the president of the Iowa Chapter and, from there, incredibly, a part of Operation Babylift. Had someone not baked those cupcakes, "a single candle," I wouldn't have been a part of that life-changing humanitarian effort. Every effort makes a difference in ways we'll likely never realize.

Balance volunteering: After my unexpected dramatic adventure with Operation Babylift, I didn't volunteer for big national causes for a while. I focused on my family while working part time and volunteered for smaller projects, like my kids' Girl Scout troops, 4H, religious ed programs, and classrooms. In an effort to achieve more life balance, mostly I just baked the cupcakes.

Chapter 19
Wise People by LeAnn

I always loved my nephew, Brian's calls sharing his family's antics and stories. One evening I sipped my coffee and put my feet up as he recounted that night's family dinner conversation with his son. "Buddy, tell me about your day."

Austin smeared gravy from his face with the back of his hand and recounted tales of his preschool adventures that day, from sandboxes to slippery slides. After swallowing his last bite of mashed potatoes, he added, "And tomorrow, we get to go see the wise people."

"Wise people?" Brian questioned.

"Yes, the wise people," Austin nodded, bouncing up and down in his chair. "I've got a paper for you to sign."

After helping to clear the table, Austin rummaged through his Sesame Street backpack and produced the crumpled permission slip. Brian smiled, "Buddy, tomorrow you get to visit a nursing home."

"Yes!" Austin beamed. "We get to go visit the old wise people."

This preschool teacher taught me:

Honor and engage with our elderly. Growing up, I spent lots of time with my grandma and loved her dearly. Yet, when I became a nurse, I preferred caring for little kids and new moms. One summer, I worked for a temp agency that assigned me to a nursing home. At first, I was less than enthused about the job, but by the end of summer, I didn't want to leave. When I took time to listen, I was enthralled with these seniors, their stories, and life lessons. I learned that old people are truly wise people.

Today, in my writings and conversations, I frequently share the philosophy of Native American tribal communities, which view their elders as collective treasure troves of cultural knowledge, experience, wisdom, stories, and insightful perspectives. Becoming an elder – not just older – isn't about attaining a certain age; it's an intentional pursuit, dedicating their lives to gaining wisdom to share with everyone in the tribe. Wisdom isn't wielded as a weapon, and experience isn't shared to glorify one's journey. Elders devote themselves to bettering their tribe with humility and benevolence. Contrarily, our society seems to worship youth, beauty, and new things while discarding less attractive things from the past. Our world will be much better when we learn to engage with the wise people who teach us so much about life. As my hair turns silver, I can hardly wait.

Chapter 20
I Can't; It Hurts Too Much by LeAnn

Other than playing hospital with my little sisters with my toy doctor's kits, I'd had no experience with nursing. Yet here I was, a first-year nursing student, fresh out of high school, eagerly and clearly called to this profession. Enthralled with anatomy, physiology, and all my classes, I couldn't wait to begin actual patient care. However, my starched white uniform and cap didn't hide my naivete and lack of experience when I was assigned my first patients.

My polished white shoes squeaked down the hall as I scurried to report to Mrs. Gowdy, my instructor. "Mrs. Jones just had surgery yesterday and doesn't want to get out of bed today because it hurts too much," I told her. "So maybe we can wait until tomorrow."

"Don't kill her with kindness, LeAnn."

I frowned, confused. "And my other patient won't cough every hour like the doctor ordered because it pulls on his incision too much."

This kind woman repeated sternly, "Don't kill him with kindness. Failure to walk and cough will cause lung congestion, pneumonia, and possibly fatal illnesses, and while it may feel unkind, remember the important outcomes from these uncomfortable activities."

I learned later in my career that it was not at all beneficial to say to a woman about to deliver a baby, "That's okay; you don't have to push if it hurts." Or to an amputee with a new prosthesis, "You don't have to stand and walk if it's uncomfortable; you can just stay in a wheelchair... for the rest of your life."

Instead, in my work and conversations today, I say, "You can do this. You're stronger than you think. It's critically important for your well-being. And I will help you."

Mrs. Gowdy taught me:

Don't kill them with kindness: This lesson applies not only in nursing but in parenting. When my toddler turned her nose up at certain foods, I wanted to say, "That's okay; fruits, vegetables and a balanced diet aren't that important." When my junior high daughter didn't want to go to school and be teased, everything in me wanted to lavish kindness on her and say, "That's okay, honey, you don't have to go if you're uncomfortable." Or in my friend's approach with her adult child. "It's okay if you don't want to get a job. It's hard out there. You can just stay home and live in the basement." Loving people and caring for them takes strength… for the caregiver and the recipient.

Chapter 21
Our "Stuff" by LeAnn

"Oh, I love the mural of the giraffe bedroom wall!" I exclaimed. "And the bright colors of all the other zoo animals."

"Yes," our realtor Moe said. "The owner of this house is quite an artist."

"This would be perfect for Angela's bedroom. What two-year-old little girl wouldn't just love this?" I patted my expectant belly. "And it would be perfect for the nursery."

"Well," Moe said, "It's several thousand dollars over your budget for your first house. Let's take a look at some of the others on our list today."

But none compared to the colorful zoo menagerie. "The one on Brookwood Drive was nice," my husband Mark offered.

"Yes, but not as nice as that first one," I sighed. "And it's within walking distance of the elementary school, and Angela will be in kindergarten in just three years. There's a playground there where we can go in the meantime, which she'll love."

Silently, we all drove back to our rented duplex to review our options.

"In order to afford this, I could work four days a week and pick up some extra shifts," I suggested hopefully.

"But honey," Mark said. "You always wanted to work just two or three days a week, which I agreed with one hundred percent, because we didn't want our little ones in childcare this early."

"Yes, I know, but maybe it would be worth it if we could have this perfect house."

Moe leaned forward and shuffled the stacks of real estate listings on our coffee table. "Yes," he said with a grim smile. "But would you own your house, or would it own you?" He went on to remind us of all the other costs of home ownership. "And there's utilities and insurance. And now you'll be responsible for all the upkeep."

I smiled and said, "Moe, I thought you'd want to sell the more expensive house to get a higher commission."

"I never want people to get in over their heads," he offered.

Angela toddled across the floor and put her head on my lap. I caressed her chubby cheek. "Let's look at the one on Brookwood Drive again tomorrow."

We bought that house on Brookwood Drive, with a school and playground in our backyard and the best neighbors and little kids we could ever hope for. Turns out that was the perfect house.

Moe, the realtor, taught me:

Don't let your "stuff" own you. To apply this life lesson, I always worked part-time (until our nest was empty, and I started my own business, worked full time, and had the toughest boss ever… me! But I digress.) While raising our family, we drove used cars, had a small ranch house, and packed sack lunches. Many families do great with both parents working full-time; every family needs to figure out what is best for them and be flexible to change it again if needed.

For me, I learned that success isn't about having more but about needing less. As I continue to wrestle with this in my life, I'm often reminded not to let my stuff own me.

PART III
MENTORS WHO MOLDED OTHERS – STORIES OF INFLUENCE, IMPACT AND BECOMING

Got joy? Gathering and reading mentorship stories from across the globe gave us joy. In a world where bad news always grabs the headline, you'll find there is plenty of good news in the world by reading these stories of mentorship.

These mentors come from all walks of life: Business, non-profit, healthcare, academics, military and athletics. They didn't have a bunch of spare time on their hands to help others. They made the time. And because they did, they *made a difference* to be the difference in a person's life.

Mentors create a legacy. As Mark Batterson shares in his book, *Chase The Lion*, legacy isn't something you leave for someone, it's something you leave in someone. As you read these stories, you'll learn about what parents, teachers, bosses, peers, colleagues, and coaches left in others. Confidence, first opportunities, encouragement, tough love, and access to others.

We hope these stories bring you joy.

Chapter 22
You Never Know by Nido Qubein

I was the youngest of five children, and shortly after I was born in the Middle East, my father became ill. When I was six years old, he died, and my two brothers and sisters and I grew up with a single parent. While she provided for our basic survival needs, she also brought us up with a lasting sense of values. Her academic career did not go past the fourth grade, but she possessed the wisdom of ages, a wisdom she shared generously, giving us precious lessons for life and a very loving home. "You may be poor in your pocket," she told us, "but you can always be healthy in your heart."

My mother insisted that her children become educated, and one of her greatest wishes was that her youngest son pursue an education in America. So I did. When I arrived on the shores of the United States in 1966 at the age of seventeen, I had about fifty dollars in my pocket, the guidance of my older brother, and a firm commitment to get a good education.

I enrolled in the Mount Olive Junior College, later renamed the University of Mount Olive, in eastern North Carolina. I chose Mount Olive for two reasons. First, the name reminded me of the Mount of Olives in scripture, which reminded me of my home in the Middle East, and frankly, I was homesick. The second, they accepted me! For which I was (and still am) extremely grateful.

I went to Mount Olive for two years to earn an associate's degree in business. Towards the end of my second year, the school president,

Dr. Burkette Raper, requested I meet with him. When I arrived in his office, he congratulated me on my fine academic work and said, "Nido, I know you *think* you paid your way through college last year." What did he mean? Of course, I had. I'd worked very hard, seven to eight-hour days, while keeping up my course load. I'd found jobs at the school and in the city and spoke at churches, making maybe ten dollar a speech. I put every penny beyond my bare living costs into tuition.

"The truth is," he continued, "there was a gap between what you paid and what you owed." He paused. "A significant gap." This startled me. The idea that I had not fulfilled my obligation was deeply troubling. Before I could say anything, he continued, "I thought you might like to know, a doctor who lives nearby picked up the tab for the difference."

I was stunned. Someone I didn't even know had paid my tuition deficit for me. "Sir, who is this doctor? I'd like to express my gratitude for his or her kindness and generosity."

"Well, Nido, I can't tell you that because this person prefers to remain anonymous. I just thought you'd like to know."

I went back to my dorm room, knelt by the side of my bed, and cried my eyes out. Right then, I made a commitment to God and to myself. As soon as I was able, the moment I began earning money beyond my own tuition and basic living expenses, I would help other people go to college, just as I had been helped.

I eventually went on to earn a master's degree in business, founded several successful businesses and eventually, at the age of fifty-six, I became President of High Point University. We serve over 6,300 students and have replaced the word "teacher," with "mentor," or the "enabler of learning."

My anonymous donor taught me:

Remember who lifted you and lift others. One of my first actions upon graduating with my master's degree was to take the first 500 dollars I could scrape together and start the Nido Qubein

Associates Scholarship Foundation. At the foundation, we never saddle our grant recipients with burdensome contracts or obligations. Our only stipulation upon awarding someone a scholarship is that they use their education and good fortune to help others like themselves.

To this date this fund has invested millions in scholarships to hundreds of students. I'm eternally grateful to all my friends who pitch in annually to make it all possible. Like me, they believe firmly what Scottish theologian William Barclay once said, "Always give without remembering; always receive without forgetting."

NIDO QUBEIN enjoys an international reputation as a dynamic speaker, much-in-demand business advisor, a respected member of national corporate boards and a university president. He's authored many books on communication and personal development and has been featured widely in national publications. He has received many prestigious awards and distinctions.

Chapter 23
She Didn't Let Me Off the Hook
by Karen Short

I was about a month into my accidental sales career when my boss looked me in the eye and said, "This isn't working."

I swallowed hard.

"I thought you knew what you were doing."

I blinked.

"I thought I did, too."

That was the beginning—and somehow, not the end.

It was 1983, and I had just landed a job as a catering coordinator with Omni Hotels. I was "herding cats" managing multiple vendors, logistics, and menu planning. One afternoon, my boss, Judi Lages, a respected powerhouse in heels, with a reputation for running a tight, accountable sales team pulled me aside.

"I think you'd be great in sales."

"Sales?" I was flattered and didn't really know what questions to ask so I said yes.

The next thing I knew, I was in the deep end of the pool, looking at a stack of client folders with directions to start calling these people to find out what upcoming events they had that we might be able to service.

That was it. No manual. No script. No "Sales for Dummies." Just figure it out.

So, I did what any self-respecting, mildly panicked newbie would do. I leaned hard on the kindness and expertise of my colleagues. Even with their help, my sales calls sounded more like an apology than a business conversation. A month later, Judi sat down with me and said, "This isn't working."

She could've cut me loose. I wouldn't have blamed her. I'd already been fired from a sales role once before—same story: no training, just a phone book, and a wish. That failure still stung.

But Judi didn't give up on me. "You've got potential," she said. "I don't have time to train you, but I'm sending you to sales school." The sales school turned out to be Xerox's Professional Selling Skills and I was a sponge. It wasn't just "how to sell." It was how to connect. Ask the right questions. Listen more than you speak. Understand what people need—then serve it. For the first time, sales made sense. It wasn't manipulation. It was communication. And I fell in love with it.

Years later, Judi promoted me to Director of Sales in Park City, Utah. I shared one piece of advice that she gave me with every salesperson I managed. "When you walk in the door, leave your ego outside. As soon as your ego is involved, you're failing. Listen, be present, and put the customer first." (I've repeated that line so many times it should be stitched on a pillow.) That advice stuck with me—especially in negotiations. The ego makes people dig in and resist. But if you're open, progress happens.

I loved my new job. It came with a gorgeous view, a big title—and reports. Lots of reports. And I started slipping again. My reporting habits? Let's just say... creative. Late. Sometimes a little messy.

"I'm just not into numbers," I told Judi one day. "It's not my strength."

A pause. And then, "I'll be there tomorrow." Sure enough, she flew out. No fanfare, no lecture. She just rolled up her sleeves and sat next to me at the desk. We worked side by side, day and night.

"You're overcomplicating it," she said. "Start basic. Build from there." She taught me how to structure a report, calculate the numbers, and write commentary, skills I've used in every job since. It was both embarrassing and humbling. But I was so grateful. She didn't just tell me what I was doing wrong, she taught me how to do it right. Her actions taught me more than any textbook could.

Years later, I left the company for a different opportunity, and she hired me back as a consultant. More than once, we had "what are you doing" conversations. She was honest, direct, and unflinching. Those courageous conversations defined our relationship and my leadership style.

Judy Lages taught me:

Get on the same side of the table. Whether it was building reports, negotiating with clients, or having hard conversations, Judi never loomed over me—she sat next to me. That image stuck. Today, I coach my sales leaders the same way. When they're ready to throw in the towel on a struggling rep, I ask, "Have you sat next to them yet? Remember, it's your job to coach them."

Don't give up too quickly. Judi didn't give up on me when I didn't know what I was doing, when I messed up the numbers, or when I was ready to walk away. And now, I don't give up on people either. I remind my team to find the person's strengths before writing them off. Most people aren't in the wrong company—they're just in the wrong seat.

Model the behavior. Her consistency shaped mine. She showed up. She coached. She corrected with kindness and a backbone. She didn't let me off the hook. And because of her, I stopped letting other people off the hook, too.

For over thirty years, **KAREN SHORT** has served in a range of B2B and B2C marketing, sales, and operations leadership positions. She's successfully executed aggressive growth strategies ranging from market-driven and sales-focused organizations to growth through mergers and acquisitions. She builds brands with a focus on quality, reliability, and thought leadership positioning.

Chapter 24
Attitude Adjustment by Jim Stanley

Two in the morning. No one around. The quiet was deafening as I worked on a McDonnell Douglas F–4 Phantom fighter jet at the El Torro, California Marine air station. This, my first year in the Marines, left me increasingly disillusioned seeing the waste and inefficiency of this large organization. I was a rebellious eighteen-year-old with limited life experiences, but thought I knew everything there was to know about how the world worked.

As I worked on this sophisticated electronic equipment, I muttered my time-worn mantra, "I'm so tired of tolerating this BS. I'll be a good mechanic, but otherwise I'm just going to do enough to get by."

One of the senior engineers with McDonald Douglas walked by and must have heard my grumbling. These experts were on standby to support me and other avionics specialists. We revered this group; they did "walk on water" because of their intelligence and knowledge. They knew everything about how this aircraft worked.

"Jim, hi my name is Pat. How is it going?"

This was my opening, and I wasted no time complaining and pointing out all the mismanagement of this confounded operation. "I could run this place better!"

The engineer paused and looked intently at me. "Jim, whatever stage of life or situation you're in, you have to give one hundred percent, regardless of circumstances. No organization is perfect. There will always be plenty of opportunities to find problems and complain, but successful people figure out ways to achieve despite obstacles."

A little embarrassed at my whining tirade, I mumbled, "Yes sir," and went back to working on the jet.

Back in my barracks, I plopped onto my bunk and had a talk with myself. "Okay, Jim, you have a choice to make. You can continue down your negative, complaining, dead end path or choose to do the best regardless of the situation you're in."

I chose the latter.

Instead of thinking, I'm going to do just enough to get by, I decided to do my best and excel in everything I do. I enrolled in the local college and completed two and a half years of college. I excelled in the Marine Corps, making the rank of sergeant in less than three years, a career path that often takes four.

After I left the Marines, I joined another large organization, The Department of Interior, working for the National Park Service. Once again, I observed inefficiencies, but instead of griping, I remembered the advice from the McDonald Douglas engineer, "Give one hundred percent."

The McDonald Douglas engineer taught me:

Do your best no matter the circumstances. Eventually, I started my own law practice where I made daily choices to do my best when working with clients. As someone who has been a prosecutor and criminal defense attorney, I've dealt with challenging people and cases. I worked just as hard on low level cases as high level cases.

During jury selection, I found jurors skeptical of the judicial system. And I would share with them that it's not perfect---nothing is. However, it's one of the best in the world where a jury of peers decides your fate, not a dictator or biased ruler. I always encouraged them to do their best. Who knew a five-minute conversation could make such an impact?

JIM STANLEY is a retired attorney with broad life experiences. Prior to practicing law, he served as a crewman on helicopter search and rescue teams with the U.S. National Park Service, was a wild land firefighter with the U.S. Department of Interior and sergeant in the U.S. Marine Corps.

Chapter 25
This Is Me by Adenike Saliu

I'll never forget the first time I met Jen Janz. At the time, I was simply looking for a way to become certified as a CNA through CrossPurpose, a non-profit located in Denver with a mission of abolishing economic and spiritual poverty through career development.

But Jen looked at me, really looked at me—and saw something more.

"You're too advanced for CNA," she said. "Why don't you go for the Medical Assistant program instead?"

I remember staring at the course work which included anatomy and physiology. "This is too much," I told her. "I don't think I can do it."

Jen smiled and said something I'll never forget: "I believe you can. In fact, I think this is exactly what you're meant to do."

And just like that, I changed my course. I graduated with certifications in medical assistance and phlebotomy. Looking back, I now ask myself, "What was I afraid of?" Thank goodness Jen believed in me before I believed in myself.

My journey didn't start in Denver. I emigrated from Nigeria in 2018 with my two youngest daughters. I left behind an emotionally difficult marriage with a military officer. I knew if I wanted a better life for myself and children and I would need to go to a country where I could start over. I filed for asylum, and three years later, it was granted.

During those early years, I was navigating a new country, parenting on my own, and unsure of where to go or who to trust.

That's when a Christian sister of mine handed me a flyer from CrossPurpose. "Maybe this is for you," she said. That simple gesture changed everything.

At Cross Purpose, I not only found a training program, I found community and I found Jen. She became my coach, my advocate, and a teacher who led with experience and empathy. She taught us using stories and videos. One day, she showed a clip from *The Greatest Showman*—the song "This Is Me." It's the story of a group of outcasts in the circus who come together to celebrate their uniqueness and defy the negativity they face from society. It wrecked me in the best way.

Jen told us not to hide our past, because our past shapes our purpose. Until then, I'd carried a quiet shame about my story, what I'd been through, what I'd left behind. But she said, "Don't be afraid to tell people what you've been through. That's when and where the healing starts."

I've held that truth in my heart ever since.

My journey has not been easy. After some housing challenges, two Cross Purpose Allies, Henry and Mary Hendrickson, invited me and my daughters to live in their basement. Allies are dedicated to walking alongside participants in a mutual mentorship relationship, and walk with me they did. We stayed there for three years. That safe space gave me time to rebuild, study, and eventually… buy a condo of my own.

With continued support from Cross Purpose and a scholarship recommendation from Jen, I went on to earn my Master's in Healthcare Leadership. This year, I am applying for an administrative fellowship program. Me, the woman who once doubted if she could even become a medical assistant.

My children often look at me and say, "Mom, who would believe all you've done?" I tell them it's all God—and it's also the people He placed in my path. From Nigeria to home ownership to a Masters in a matter of just a handful of years is because of great people like the Hendrickson's and Jen Janz who allowed me to flourish.

Jen, Henry and Mary taught me:

Rise to your own potential. Surround yourself with people who believe in you and will invest time in helping you become "your best self." Find those people who say the right words at the right time because they can and will change the direction of your life.

Your past isn't a stain. Don't hide your past because your past is part of your future. Don't be ashamed of your scars: they are a sign they you are healing or have been healed. Don't let anyone or anything break you down.

ADENIKE SALIU is a medical assistant lead at the University of Colorado Hospital Aurora with a master's degree in healthcare leadership and hoping to get into the Administrative fellowship program at the Hospital.

Chapter 26
What Am I Doing Here? by Allison Schmitt

I was at Olympic training camp training alongside some of the greatest swimmers in the world...people with records, medals, and contracts.

There was a day at camp when I just felt completely out of my depth. I couldn't hit my intervals. Everything felt heavier than it should. "What am I doing here? I don't belong. I'm not good enough."

And then Michael walked over. Michael Phelps. The greatest swimmer of all time. He could have ignored me. Most would have. But he didn't.

"Hey, everything okay?"

I wear my emotions on my sleeve and at that time, I just tried to come off as positive, happy go lucky at all times. "Yeah, just one of those off days." I tossed out a joke, trying to divert the conversation.

He didn't buy it, and instead of offering a quick, "You'll be fine," he provided real encouragement. He opened up, sharing rough patches he'd been through. "You belong here," he said. "You're not just some outsider. You've earned this spot." That conversation changed how I viewed myself. Not just as a swimmer, but as someone worthy of being in that space, worthy of pushing toward greatness.

We didn't have this official proclamation that he'd be my mentor. It didn't happen because we were on the same team training together. It happened because he saw potential in me and proactively reached out to help me through the steps of becoming an Olympic champion. And those steps happened in moments.

He'd bring me into conversations.

Share a laugh when I needed it.

Encourage and believe in me during a tough practice set.

And most of all, he was always a steady presence. He didn't just show up when it was easy to celebrate; he showed up when it was hard to keep going. He was there through the day-to-day work, the ups and downs, the mundane, daily practices. No journey to the top is a straight line and Michael zigzagged with me.

Michael's mentorship wasn't only in the words he said, it was also how he lived. He was relentless about visualization. He didn't just picture winning; he visualized the entire race---how it would feel to dive in, how his stroke would feel at the 150, even how his goggles might fill with water. Watching him taught me that preparation isn't just about muscle; it's about mindset. Success doesn't start on race day; it starts in your mind, in the moments when no one is watching. That discipline, level of intentionality, accountability permanently changed my approach to preparation.

He also modeled consistency, focus, and commitment by how he handled pressure, adversity, and even personal struggles. Never pretending to be perfect, he let me, and others see the full picture. The human side. That kind of vulnerability, paired with his work ethic, taught me how to lead.

Michael always had this uncanny ability to read me. When my motivation was fading or I wasn't fully locked in, he'd push the right buttons, challenging me, reminding me of what I was capable of, and not allowing me to coast. He held me to a high standard because he knew what it took to compete at the highest level.

Another time when I was going through some mental struggles, he was brave enough to say, "That's not like you. What's going on?" That question was enough. It made me pause, look inward, and ask for help. He saw me---not just as an athlete, but a person.

Michael taught me:

Presence is powerful. Sometimes all it takes is someone seeing you, really seeing you. I've achieved more in this sport than I ever thought possible. Not just in terms of medals or accomplishments, but in how I show up as a human being. Michael's encouragement, "walking the talk," and the way he treated me made me feel like I belonged. Today, I strive to do that for others.

Kindness is a lifeline. You never know what Chapter of life someone is in. I've been the person in the room who looked fine on the outside and felt completely alone on the inside. I know how heavy it can be to feel surrounded by the noise but still unseen. Sometimes the most powerful thing you can offer someone isn't advice, a solution, or a plan. It's your belief in them, especially when they've forgotten how to believe in themselves.

Be the grounded voice in chaos. As a mentor, I strive not just to give answers but to help people reconnect with themselves. I remind them to trust their voice, honor what they need and know, and recognize their worth has nothing to do with their "time or medals."

ALLISON SCHMITT is a four-time U.S. Olympian, ten-time Olympic medalist, and passionate mental health advocate. With a master's in social work and as Chief Empowerment Officer of SURGE, powered by BSN SPORTS, she champions confidence, resilience, and authenticity—empowering the next generation to lead, grow, and pursue greatness in and beyond sport.

Chapter 27
The Rookie and a Hundred Lessons
by Chris Younger

"If Jim gets the job, I want to go work for him, even if it means taking a pay cut," I told my wife at dinner. I worked for an investor group that owned a communications company, and we interviewed Jim Walker for the CEO role. Within the first hour, I knew I wanted to work for him. I believed I'd learn more from him about leadership, management, and strategy than I could from any high salary position. And I was right.

Jim started me off overseeing strategy and marketing, and later he promoted me to COO and eventually President. From managing a team of four or five to leading 4,200 people, it was a leap. But I didn't take it alone. My office was right next to his, and I can't count how many times I walked in with a challenge and walked out with clarity.

One such time happened during the trifecta of 9/11, Y2K, and a market crash. Sales and profits were not where they needed to be, plus there were challenges with personnel. As a young manager, I was nervous and anxious. "Chris, if we have a problem and a plan, we have no stress. If we have a problem and no plan, we have stress. Let's work on the plan."

On the morning of the 9/11 tragedy, I arrived in the office early, but Jim was already there, calm and focused, building a plan. He immediately got the entire company on a call and located our team members in Manhattan and D.C. "We're not sure what's happening or why it's happening. My first concern is the team. Do we know where everyone is? How about their families?"

Prior to the call, I had been panicking about the business. Jim showed me how to focus on the right thing… the people. That day, I saw servant leadership at its highest level.

Before Jim's mentorship, I delayed tough conversations. Jim leaned into them. He didn't see them as necessary evils, but opportunities to strengthen relationships and resolve thorny issues. He taught me how to conduct exit interviews. Those are hard conversations, ones I'm tempted to avoid until I hear Jim's voice. "Do the hard things for the good of the team."

Jim helped me battle the monster called imposter syndrome. I was the youngest member of our executive team by about fifteen years, and when I made a mistake, Jim didn't sugarcoat it. He called one of my blunders "a rookie mistake." It stung, but he was right. And I grew from it.

We once traveled the country giving updates to employees during a tough financial year. After one of my presentations, where I had just received some difficult news from a lender, he pulled me aside and said, "If you give another presentation like that, I'm going to have to fire you. Your words were fine," he said, "but your body language broadcasted fear and uncertainty." That day, he taught me that people don't just listen to a leader's words, they watch the leader's face. They feel the leader's energy, and they mirror it.

Before working for Jim, I focused on *my* performance. I wasn't patient with people who "got in the way." Jim flipped that mindset. He helped me see that people aren't in the way, they *are* the way. I had pushed people hard, sometimes too hard, and a few left because of it. During one conversation, Jim reminded me, "Chris, team members are essentially volunteers. You don't demand their best, you earn it by enlisting them in a shared vision. People implement best that which they helped create."

Jim taught me:

Take care of the people. As the CEO of my own company, I carry around a Book of Jim's 100 Lessons, figuratively speaking, but honestly, I could probably write one literally. Our entire business strategy today is a page out of his playbook: take care of the team first. Great teams take care of customers, and customers take care of shareholders.

Be self-aware. When I walk into my office each day, I think of his words. "The organization takes its cue on how it should feel about the business based on how the employees perceive you're feeling. They watch your body language, energy, tonality and optimism." No matter the pressures I'm carrying, I try to bring positive energy and a belief in the future. Both are contagious and it's how you build great cultures.

CHRIS YOUNGER is the CEO and Co-Founder of Class VI Partners, a twenty year-old financial services firm in Denver serving entrepreneurs in the U.S. Prior to Class VI, he was the President of Expanets, the nation's largest communications value-added reseller. He is a graduate of Miami University and Harvard Law School.

Chapter 28
You Can Do This by Jerry Van Leuven

In eighth grade, I decided to run for junior high student body vice president in Granger, Utah. Although I was a nerd competing against a popular athlete whose dad was well-connected in local politics, my heart was set. I decided to put my best foot forward and go for it!

After days of hard work and campaigning, the time finally arrived for the election winners to be announced. Our principal turned on the intercom and tapped the microphone, as he did before each end-of-the-day announcement. I looked down and held my breath. "Our next year's student body vice president is..." not my name. My stomach turned. I had lost. I was so ashamed. When the final bell rang, I slipped deftly out of my algebra class and headed straight out the front doors so I didn't have to see or talk to another soul.

As I walked across the front lawn, I looked up and saw a familiar orange station wagon. Frank. My scoutmaster was waiting for me. Unbeknownst to me, he had called the school ahead to learn who had won the election. He wanted to either celebrate my victory or console my broken heart.

The window rolled down. "Hey Jerry, come with me; let's go for a ride."

"No, Frank, I just want to be alone."

"Come on, it's not that bad."

"Really, Frank, you can go."

"I'll take you for some ice cream. Come on, get in."

I kept walking, and he kept slowly trailing me until I was convinced that he would not leave me alone. I finally turned around and got in his car.

Within ten minutes, I was sitting in an ice cream parlor, spooning chocolate malt into my mouth and talking about our next campout. The loss still stung, but the ice cream seemed to shrink the pain... or was it Frank?

Several months later, I reluctantly joined the rest of my scout troop at the Granger High School swimming pool, supposedly for a night of fun. But for me, it wasn't going to be fun. Hanging out in the shallow kids' pool was embarrassing. I'd nearly drowned a few years earlier in the deep end of another pool and silently vowed never to find myself in the same situation.

Suddenly, Frank appeared. "Come on, Jerry, let's go over to the deep end, and I'm going to teach you how to jump in."

"I will never do that, Frank. I almost drowned once you know."

"I've got a trick to help you overcome your fear. Let's go."

"No way, Frank."

This time, it took a lot more convincing to talk me into doing something I didn't want to do. But there was something about Frank. I trusted him. I knew he cared about me. So, I followed him.

I stood on the side of the deep end as Frank got into the pool. "Will you jump into my arms if I stay real close to the side and catch you?"

"No."

After much cajoling, I finally sat down on the edge... then slowly slipped into the terrifying, deep, chlorinated water. It took my breath away. It was scary. But there, safe in Frank's grasp, it was pretty cool. Frank told me to climb out and then positioned himself a foot further away from the edge.

"Okay, Jerry, I want you to do the same thing. I promise I will catch you, turn you around and push you back to the side."

Lips blue and teeth chattering, I hesitated for a long time. Then it happened. I suddenly jumped toward Frank, knowing he would save me. We repeated this over and over and over. Within an hour, Frank had me jumping off the diving board, first next to where he was treading water, and eventually plunging into the deep water all by myself and doggy paddling to the side. It was exhilarating. I was on top of the world. Pure victory. And all because of Frank.

As a sixty-one-year-old, I've reflected many times on this ordinary man's incredibly positive impact on my life. As an awkward kid, learning to figure out who I was, trying to love and believe in myself, I watched Frank cross my path in critical moments. He wasn't handsome, his hands were rough from years of manual labor, and he and his wife LaVon were raising their own large family of kids. But I knew Frank loved me. He helped me set up my first hi-fi stereo system in my bedroom. He and LaVon had an open-door weekend night policy for any teenage boy who wanted to spend a night playing cards, eating big bowls of ice cream, and laughing until it hurt. He started my lifetime fascination of raising tropical fish. Frank was there when I graduated from high school, left home for college, served a church mission, and finally married and moved across the country.

In time, I flew back home with my family and took my two young boys to Frank's house for as much ice cream as they wanted, and we all laughed until it hurt.

Frank taught me:

Help teenagers. Today, I run a nonprofit with a mission to create youth interactions that strengthen resilience and leadership to help teens prevent mental health crises. I invite adult volunteers to spend time mentoring them on a ranch where they can breathe country air, get outside themselves by caring for a goat or a mini horse, and be present with an adult who isn't there to diagnose them but keeps showing up week after week.

Unlike kids today, I didn't grow up with a mobile phone and social media barraging me with messages of "I'm not good enough" and threats of not being socially safe. My simple world included seeing my parents tune in to Walter Cronkite every night at 5:00 p.m. and agreeing with the rest of America on everything he said. I played kick-the-can until late at night and learned how to really connect and communicate with my friends face to face.

But I still needed someone to reinforce my value and help me to feel secure.

I needed a male mentor to challenge me and push me out of my comfort zone.

Those moments with Frank were gold. The rough hands, the ice cream, the "Come on Jerry, you can do this" encouragement all worked together to propel me into manhood, fatherhood, and ultimately, a late professional career that allows me to turn around and pay it forward.

JERRY VAN LEUVEN founded The Aspen Effect in 2017 to prevent youth mental health crisis and substance use disorder. With the help of adult volunteer mentors, a herd of seventy horses and other farm animals, they currently serve over 240 youth. Find out more by going to www.theaspeneffect.org.

Chapter 29
You Don't Have the Full Picture
by Sarah Kiley

I didn't show up to the job looking for a mentor. I showed up just trying to keep my head above water.

It was my first month at a scrappy edtech startup with about forty employees. We were small but ambitious. They brought me on to explore new markets beyond the usual K–12 and higher ed lanes. Uncharted territory for them. And new territory for me.

Most days felt like I was sprinting while still tying my shoes. I was too focused on staying afloat to think about things like mentorship.

That's when I met John Reese.

John was the founding CEO, now chairman of the board. He was several rungs up the org chart from where I sat as a sales rep. But from day one, he noticed me. He had this quiet but unmistakable belief in me. He shared insights, helped me navigate new global markets, and most importantly he made time between board meetings and global travel. Not hours, just minutes here and there. A quick call. No official check-ins or formal development plan but a whole lot of support.

There was one conversation I'll never forget.

I'd spent weeks building a strategic global partnership—early morning calls across time zones, late-night decks, the whole nine yards. I was ready to present my solutions and had earned my seat at the table. When it came time for the formal meeting, my boss told me that he'd be going instead.

I was devastated. I'd done all the groundwork. This wasn't fair.

About that time, I received a call from John. "So how are things going?" I let it all out. "I spent weeks on this partnership and now I'm being sidelined. Honestly, I'm wondering if I even belong here."

I expected a pep talk or some sort of righteous validation. Instead, John told me a story. "Sarah, years ago, early in my career, I was passed over for a big promotion. I was furious and stormed into my boss's office to plead my case. My boss listened, let me vent, then said something that changed my perspective. *'John, your view is limited to what you know. And what you know isn't the full picture.'*

That story hit me like a ton of bricks. John wasn't brushing me off—he was reframing how I saw the situation. "Assume you don't have the full picture. Lead with humility, ask questions, and listen."

A couple of weeks later, I was on a work trip with our CEO. I took a deep breath and said, "I know I might not have the full picture, but based on what I know, this is frustrating. Can you help me understand why my boss is leading that meeting instead of me?"

He listened. He didn't rush to respond, but he made me feel heard. A few days later, my boss stepped aside. "You've built the momentum," he told me. "You should lead it."

And just like that, I was back on the project, and yes, I landed the business. That conversation didn't just change the trajectory of that deal—it changed how I lead.

John Reese taught me:

Slow down and get the full picture. I coach others to assume they don't have the full picture. One woman I recently mentored felt that decisions being made above her were limiting her success. I shared John's advice, word for word. Today, she's a VP of Sales and Marketing. Funny how perspective unlocks potential.

Mentorship doesn't always require hours of time. Years later, when I was promoted to GM, John was the first to call. "This is what I always envisioned for you," he said. He still checks in and makes time. I've learned that if you can make a phone call while your coffee brews, you can mentor. Blocking thirty minutes for a conversation on a Friday afternoon can change a life.

SARAH KILEY is a revenue leader known for building high-performing teams, mentoring future leaders, and driving customer-centric growth. With deep experience in SaaS, education, and AI-powered solutions, she brings grit, heart, and strategic vision to every role. She's passionate about empowering others and shaping the future of sales leadership.

Chapter 30
Resilient by Rolanda Pyle

I sat looking out my window, wondering, how in the world did we get here? I sighed as I saw the empty streets of New York City, one of the busiest places in the U.S., and not a soul to be seen. During the Covid–19 pandemic, we were on lockdown and quarantined to contain the spread of the worldwide virus.

I shook my head, and thought, when will this end? This pandemic was extremely difficult for me because I am not a stay-at-home person. I love going out to enjoy all the aspects of the city, especially in this springtime. Living alone, with no one to see and talk to, was wearing on my body, mind, and spirit. How long will this go on?

I blew out a deep breath. Time to sign in and start my remote workday. Usually, my job entailed outreach for my program, CARENYC, which assists caregivers of someone with Alzheimer's/dementia. But, due to the trying times, I'd been asked to assist the Friendly Visiting program and conduct daily check-in calls to seniors.

Taking one last yearning look out the window, I envisioned the bustling streets I longed for and prayed that someday things would be back the way they used to be.

I pulled out my list and began calling the seniors. I heard cries of despair, loneliness, concern, and resiliency. I identified with some of what they were going through and as I comforted them, I found comfort too.

My frowns turned to smiles as I heard uplifting stories of survival. One man told me this reminded him of his battles fighting in the Korean War. He said, "I will use the same strength I used in the war to help me as I cope with this pandemic."

Another woman offered, "I will get through this because I grew up in the racist South. I saw lynchings. You cannot imagine the terror I felt just walking down the street. I made it through that and despite Jim Crow laws, I experienced the civil rights movement. So, I know, with the help of God, I will make it through this, too."

Still, another recalled, "This is nothing compared to what I went through during the Holocaust." Her frail voice continued, "If I can survive that, then I can survive anything. It's one thing to have to stay in for the safety of yourself and others, but it is another thing to have to stay in and hide with your family because you don't want anyone to know you are there. Because if they do know, they will come to get you and imprison or kill you."

Wow, I thought to myself. *This wisdom puts things in perspective.* Although this time was hard for me, so many seniors had made it through much more difficult life-threatening situations.

As I reflected on these stories of war, racism, isolation, hiding, quarantine, and hate, I realized the source of their resiliency was found in strength, faith, family, trust in God, and the will to fight.

I was inspired knowing that after the pandemic, we all had stories to tell. Now we realize what is important.

These courageous seniors taught me:

Keep things in perspective. I love and respect seniors more because of what they have lived through; I am more grateful for the things I took for granted and thank God for life and the ability to fulfill my purpose. Like these wise sages, I encourage others to use the 2020 pandemic experiences to better our lives and the world. All things work together for good and because of that, we can keep the faith, stay strong, trust God and we, too, will be resilient.

ROLANDA T. PYLE is a licensed social worker in the field of aging. She is the author of four books: *FINALLY, Beneath His Everlasting Wings, Grandma's Hands* and *ALL THINGS.* She is a contributor to many journals, anthologies, magazines, collections, devotionals and other publications.

Chapter 31
The Mentor Who Caught on Fire
by Steve Spangler

In line at the Denver International Airport, I heard laughter erupting near the United counter. I didn't even have to look.

"Here, let me show you my ID," the sixty year-old man said to the United Airlines gate attendant as he retrieved his wallet from his hip pocket. When he opened it, fiery flames shot up!

"Yikes!" squealed the gate attendant.

The man slammed his wallet shut, the flames disappeared, and his chuckle turned to deep laughter. She chuckled hesitantly.

"Oh, Carol, I just wanted to make you smile today. You do such a wonderful job and what you do is so important."

Then Earl Reum turned to me and asked, "Steven Douglas Spangler, where are you going?" Earl was the only one who called me by my full name and every time he did, I couldn't help but smile. "You got your fire wallet?" he asked.

"No, Earl," I said. "That's your trick." He placed his wallet in my hand... the legendary wallet with worn edges and cracked leather, softened by years of sparking wonder in crowds big and small. "This has served me well for thirty-five years," he said. "Now it's yours. Promise me you'll keep it fueled. You never know who needs a smile. And remember, it's not about the fire. It's about the connections you create."

I was five years old when I first met Earl Reum, a man who could make books burst into flames, levitate objects, and vanish scarves only to have them reappear moments later. But beyond the tricks and illusions, what really grabbed me wasn't the magic, it was the joy Earl sparked in the people around him. Joy, connection, laughter. That was Earl's real magic.

I grew up in a family of professional magicians. My parents, Bruce and Kitty Spangler, traveled the country with a magic act that took off in the 1970s. My siblings and I were always part of the show, whether we were hiding in secret compartments or pulling off tricks of our own. Magic wasn't just a weekend thing, it was our way of life

Our house in Denver headquartered for one of the largest magic schools in the western United States. That meant we had a steady stream of magicians, both aspiring and seasoned, coming through. And Earl? He was one of the regulars. He'd stop by to drop off a book for our library or chat with students newly discovering the world of magic.

My dad taught most of the famous magicians, including David Copperfield. But Earl Reum taught me lessons my dad did not.

When I was in ninth grade, I called him to ask if he'd speak at our school's leadership conference. I knew there was no way we could afford someone like Earl.

"I have that day blocked out for you," he said. "And don't worry, it's covered by a special grant. This is our way of celebrating you and your presidency at Goddard Middle School. Can't wait to see you!"

Of course, there was no grant. Earl never let something like money get in the way of a good teaching moment. That day, I stood in the back of the room and watched him hold the entire audience in the palm of his hand, not with tricks, but with truths. I watched what he did to everybody. Earl started with the old-style magic ropes trick I'd seen one hundred times.

"This small rope is you, the person," he said waving an eight-inch rope. "And it's touching the middle side of this bigger rope which is all of the people who are important in your life." With a snap of his wrist, the two ropes became one. My classmates oohed and aahed. "And that connection could never be more important than today on March 11th of the year 1981. I'm here to tell you that the greatest secrets in life aren't secrets at all," he said. "They're right in front of you. You just need a new perspective. Life is about connections. Look someone in the eye and say thank you. That's how you build a better world."

That moment changed everything for me. I didn't just want to be a magician. Or a teacher. I wanted to create the kind of moments that connected people, to science, to wonder, and to each other.

As I watched Earl, I realized why he always wore a suit… he needed all those pockets, for the gags, tricks, and surprises to have ready at every moment. And I'll never forget the smell. Earl always had a faint scent of lighter fluid clinging to him. He loved fire tricks. His flaming book and wallet delighted unsuspecting waiters and hotel clerks. Forks squeaked, wine glasses vanished, and once he even produced a live chicken at the front desk of a Marriott.

But the tricks were never the point. Earl used magic as a tool to open hearts and minds. He wasn't trying to impress people, he was trying to connect them. His greatest trick? Turning strangers into participants and bystanders into believers.

In 1948, *Life* magazine named him one of the top emerging student leaders in the country. While teaching junior high English in Denver, he earned his doctorate in education with a focus on student leadership. His work helped shape the way student leadership programs are run across the country even to this day. Earl held a full-time job as Director of Student Activities for Jefferson County Schools, yet he still found time to travel and speak at student leadership conferences across the country. He used his life as a laboratory to spark passion and purpose in young people.

Because I loved magic, it made sense that I studied chemistry and became a teacher. But, thanks to Earl, I wanted to make an even greater impact.

One Saturday morning I left a message on his answering machine. "Hi Earl. I just need to talk to you about becoming a leadership speaker. What do you think?" Beep. I hung up

When I came home later, I had a message on my answering machine. "Oh, Stephen Douglas Spangler, listen. I've been thinking about how the world needs to hear your message. I need you and your lovely wife Renee in New Orleans. I'm going to send you some plane tickets. I'm going to have you talk to some of my friends. I'll see you on December 5th."

Three days later the tickets showed up. When we arrived in New Orleans, Earl had arranged for me to speak to hundreds of people at the National Association for Student Activities, an organization he founded. I gave a terrible speech, but with Earls tutelage, it filled my calendar for the next ten years.

Over the years Earl and I had many meetings on his front porch. On one of those lovely breezy afternoons, Earl turned to me and said, "I need you to carry the torch for me, Stephen Douglas Spangler. I can't do this forever. You've got to carry it because a lot of people need to know that they got seen that day and that somebody thought they made a difference in their life."

Earl passed away in December of 2010. In those final months, we spent hours on his front porch, swapping stories, revisiting old tricks, and imagining the future.

Weeks later, as I helped his beloved wife sort the 20,000 books and thousands of magic tricks stuffed inside their tiny home, we discovered keys to two secret storage units. Inside, crammed from front to back, floor to ceiling, were hundreds of boxes of magic tricks. I knew Earl didn't need any of them; he'd only ordered them to "see and recognize and thank" the vendors who sold them.

Earl Reum helped me figure out who I was—as a teacher, a speaker, a husband, and a dad. But more than anything, he showed me what it means to mentor. He gave me the tools to pass it on, to lead with joy, to teach through wonder, and to connect with people in ways that really matter.

Earl Reum taught me:

It's not about the magic, but the message. Earl showed me how to use wonder to invite people in. That idea, that joy and curiosity are essential to engagement, shaped how I teach, how I speak, and how I try to show up for people every day. He often reminded me that people don't always remember what you said as much as how you made them feel. Earl's superpower was his ability to connect with and honor everybody he met. Thanks to Earl, I've hosted several educational science TV shows. He called me laughing when my Diet Coke and Mentos eruption experiment went viral in 2005. Eventually I had a warehouse crammed from front to back, floor to ceiling with hundreds of boxes of science magic tricks, to help kids, teachers and leaders. And Earl smiled down from heaven when I used a flaming torch… his torch… to blow up pumpkins on the Ellen DeGeneres show.

If you saw the enormous mess **STEVE SPANGLER** repeatedly made on the Ellen Show over the past fifteen years, you'll understand why Ellen calls Steve… the science teacher you always wanted to have in school because the fire department shows up twice a year. For more information, visit SteveSpangler.com.

Chapter 32
Be on Time, Be Ready by Matt Mitchell

"You're late. Start running."

Those were the first words Coach Permakoff shouted when anyone showed up five minutes late for baseball practice.

No hello. No warm-up. Just consequences.

At the time, it felt a little extreme. I mean, really, five minutes.

But the Coach wasn't just trying to break us down, he was trying to build something. And I didn't fully understand that until much later.

I grew up loving sports. I loved the competition, the camaraderie, the thrill of the game. But more than anything, sports taught me discipline. This focus on discipline was also reinforced by two other key influences in my life, my dad and uncle.

When I was young, my grandfather passed away unexpectedly. He had built a respected electrical contracting business from the ground up. After he passed, my dad and uncle, both still young themselves, stepped in to run the company. I didn't hear excuses or complaints. I did see a lot of action.

I remember many a Saturday when they'd head out to a job site before sunrise. They just didn't manage and give orders from a distance. They were in the trenches with the rest of their team, sleeves rolled up and getting their hands dirty. It left a deep impression on me: If there's work to be done, you get it done. Show up and give it everything you've got.

Then came high school baseball. Coach Permakoff. He had played and been coached in the Army. You were expected to show up early, dressed, focused, and ready. If you weren't, you paid for it. If it became a pattern, you sat out and then you were out.

He was preparing us for life, not just for nine innings.

He showed us that respect starts with how you show up for your teammates, your responsibilities, and for yourself.

That mindset stayed with me into adulthood. In business, being prepared and punctual isn't just appreciated—it's expected. Whether I'm stepping into a client meeting or leading my own team, I hear Coach's voice in my head: *"Be on time. Be ready."*

Now, as a coach myself—both in the office and on the court, I try to pass that same mindset on to others.

This past basketball season, my youth basketball team lost badly to a really strong opponent by twenty-nine points. It would've been easy to blame talent, size, or bad luck. Instead, I gathered the team and passed on the wisdom from my mentors: how you show up everyday matters. Your habits, your effort, your preparation are what positively change future outcomes.

Weeks later, we faced that same team in the playoffs… and we beat them by three.

My mentors taught me:

Winning isn't about luck. It's about discipline. It's about preparation. It's about all the little choices we make in life. Choosing to practice, show up early, give it our all and refusing to settle.

Do the Work. There will always be curveballs thrown at us in life. Instead of complaining or making excuses, do the work to change the curveball to a homerun. Don't ask anyone to do what you won't do or haven't done. Lead by example as unspoken words are often the most impactful words.

MATT MITCHELL brings energy and insight to his role leading sales operations at Playcore. With degrees from the University of Tennessee, he blends sharp business acumen with a genuine passion for people. Off the clock, Matt's happiest outdoors—chasing sports, adventures with his four kids, and the thrill of game-day wins.

Chapter 33
The 3 M's – The Mentors Who Made Me
by Shiretta Shaw

You never know when mentorship is happening. It doesn't always come with a title or a twelve month plan. Sometimes it sounds like a late-night pep talk from your mom. Other times, it's a provocative question from a colleague. And, once in a while, it's your husband handing you the push you didn't know you needed.

Looking back, the people who shaped my leadership journey fall into what I now call "The 3 M's": My Mothers, Marilyn, and Mitchell.

M #1: My Mothers

I can still hear their voices. "What God has for you is for you. Not for anyone else."

That's what my mom and Godmother would say, especially when life stung or didn't seem fair. They were women of deep faith, and that one sentence became the anchor I clung to when things didn't go my way or self-doubt started making an appearance.

It echoed in my ears during a difficult time in my career. I spent an entire year interviewing for a sales enablement role at IBM. If you've never been through an IBM interview process, imagine trying to get hired by a company you already work for, but with the intensity of a first-time candidate. Resume reviews. Panel interviews. Round after round after round.

Only to hear, "We've chosen someone else."

I was questioning my value and on the verge of giving up. That's when my mother's words came back again. "This isn't for you. What's meant for you will fit. It won't be forced."

Then came the call.

"Shiretta, I want you to come work for me. I know you, your talent, and your work ethic." It was Dean Marsh, a VP of Sales, who had seen my work and didn't need a resume to recognize it. No drawn-out interview. No over-explaining. Just recognition and a role that fits.

It wasn't rejection. It was redirection. And I was reminded of my mother and Godmothers' advice, "What God has for you is for you and you alone and no one else."

M #2: Marilyn – The Colleague Who Made Me a Leader

Marilyn Chatman wasn't a boss, but she was the person you went to when you were at a crossroads. And that's exactly where I found myself: ready to move from individual sales contributor to leader, but unsure how.

She is a wise person, has lots of stories, and pours a lot into people. She didn't coddle me and stopped me cold when she asked, "Why do you want to be in leadership?"

I fumbled. "Well… isn't that just how you move up? You get a title?"

She raised an eyebrow. I could tell she wasn't buying it. So, I sat and reflected on the question.

"I think I'm meant to help people grow. I ran study groups at Global Sales School. I've always volunteered to mentor interns. I love helping people figure things out."

That's when she smiled and followed up with leadership wisdom.

"Leadership isn't about being the smartest person in the room. It's about listening to perspectives that aren't yours. Get to know your people, their aspirations, their why. Find out what lights a fire in them.

And finally, don't carry forward old baggage. People get typecast because of a previous mistake or misconception. Give every person a fresh sheet of paper because people can change and grow."

Marilyn didn't just give advice. She modeled it.

She kept personal profiles on every direct report—birthdays, anniversaries, their kids names, goals. She celebrated life moments and professional wins. She understood that data doesn't drive performance. Connection does.

I built those same profiles for my first team. When hiring a new team member, I called their previous managers to uncover the good, the bad, and the ugly. And then, I got out a clean sheet of paper.

M #3: Mitchell – The Push to Put My Name on the Board

Then there was Mitchell. My IBM colleague. My sounding board. Eventually, my husband.

Early in my management career, I led a team of eight and found myself knee-deep in a messy restructuring. Technical sales teams were being realigned. I was trying to make sense of the puzzle—how to match skills to the right territories, how to make the whole thing work.

I was deep in prep when Mitchell looked at me and said, "I've already seen your new org chart."

Wait... what?

Turns out, decisions had already started happening—without me. There had been a meeting and conversation. And I hadn't been in the room. I was the youngest. The least experienced. The only woman. And now, the last to know.

Seeing my disappointment, Mitchell encouraged me. "Put your name on the board. When you've got a seat at the table, don't be shy about asking for what you need. You can either shrink or speak up." I chose to speak up.

At the next meeting, the available territories were laid out:

Wall Street – known as the premier accounts.

Insurance – referred to as strategic accounts.

Small-to-Mid Market – "bread and butter accounts" comprised of small to medium-sized businesses.

I wanted the small to mid-size market. It wasn't a glamorous market; however, I knew my team could really make a difference. However, I strategically said, "I want Wall Street."

Silence. Eyes widened. Then came the pushback: "That's already spoken for." "That's mine." After some healthy debate (and knowing this would be the response), I said, "Okay. I'll take small-to-mid. But here's what I'll need to make it a success. And I ticked off a list of things I required from people and resources.

And I got exactly what I asked for because I put my name on the board.

My 3 M's taught me:

Resilience is built in the waiting. When doors close, it's not rejection—it's redirection. Trust that the right doors will open.

Great leadership is personal. Lead with your heart, know your people, and always give others the gift of a clean slate.

Don't wait for permission. Speak up. Claim your seat. Put your name on the board—even if you weren't invited to the meeting.

SHIRETTA A. SHAW-WIGGINS, Americas Sales Enablement Leader at IBM, brings over thirty years of experience in technology, sales, and management. She has held numerous client-facing roles throughout her career. A passionate advocate for skills and leadership development, she drives programs that strengthen coaching and managerial effectiveness across IBM's Technology business unit.

Chapter 34
A Change of Perspective by Dave Hataj

I've spent decades trying to understand my father. His work ethic was epic as a phenomenally skilled machinist and gear maker. He sometimes worked all night for a customer whose factory was shut down because of one broken gear on a critical piece of equipment. His work ethic extended to everything he did, from sawing firewood to growing a garden. It was exhausting keeping up with him.

But like many midwestern men growing up in the shadow of the Great Depression, he was not warm and fuzzy. He had a great sense of humor, but intimate conversations were not in his wheelhouse. Feelings were simply not shared unless you had had more than a few beers, and then maybe a few moments of crying in your beer were okay. Otherwise, to be a man meant to suck it up and keep moving.

I sensed early on that something was broken in my father and his friends. I didn't realize it at the time, but most of my dad's acquaintances were alcoholics. As a child, I spent a lot of time in the local bars with Dad, as did many of my friends with their parents. He even put a quarter barrel of beer in his shop lunchroom for after-work parties every night.

This was my "normal."

In my late teens, I began to question the path my life was heading. I partied and drank heavily like most men in my extended family. It was then that I learned that my dad's dad, who passed away the year before I was born, died as a homeless person on the streets of Chicago. I wondered what it must have been like for my dad to have such a father. What had been his "normal" growing up? Was I destined to carry on the legacy of alcoholism so embedded in our family history?

At nineteen, my world was rocked by what some call a religious experience. I was depressed to the point of being suicidal and didn't see much purpose in life. While training for a marathon on an early Saturday morning run, God spoke to me. Whether an audible voice or one spoken to my heart, it simply said, "You are not alone." Shortly after, the first of two key mentors appeared, pivotal in redirecting my life path.

Enter Pete, and then Gerry. Each of them presented me with a radically new worldview. Both were men of devout faith who helped me understand that following Jesus was not about religion and going to church but living life very differently.

Pete, the son of a rodeo champion and a New York City debutant of high society, told me his story of growing up in rodeo's rough and tumble world, taking after his father. At the same time, his mother brought class and sophistication to the marriage. Family alcoholism was normal for Pete as well, until he "got religion" as a young man, as I had at nineteen. Pete invited me for breakfast or lunch and asked me how I was doing. He knew the difficulty of breaking out of my family's "normal."

I had stopped drinking and going to bars; I wanted to live a life of excellence, one foreign to my family and friends. My not drinking with them made them feel rejected and judged, exactly what I experienced from them. I felt lonely and confused, yet passionate about my newfound faith. Anyone who has ever struggled with addiction knows how difficult it is to break out of our old social groups and norms. Pete understood this. "Your new path is worth it." His look and laugh instilled confidence and hope. He always pointed out positive things I didn't see in myself. Like a desert, I soaked up every word of encouragement like life itself.

Pete was pivotal in my leaving home when I was twenty-two and moving to California. I needed to start over and be free of my old identity. After eight years, I came back home with a wife and infant son. However, if I thought leaving my life behind when I moved was difficult, returning to help Dad's business was hell.... and then it got worse. Enter Gerry.

Gerry was twenty-five years old and had only one job his entire life. He was a second-generation baker, the son of an unpredictable, sometimes terrifying, alcoholic baker. Gerry, too, had come to faith as a young man. Somehow, he navigated changing the family business culture while changing and growing himself. He knew *exactly* what I was experiencing, trying to do the same while transitioning my dad into retirement.

Those ten years almost killed me and my marriage. I came to understand that people will often fight to stay in their misery rather than risk embracing change. They also often frown upon removing their free beer by removing the quarter barrel!

Gerry met with me often but never allowed me to whine or wallow in self-pity. He coached me with his Gerry-isms: "Suck it up, Buttercup." "God always returns us to the scene of the crime." "You're always waiting for the other shoe to drop." "It hurts like hell, but what's the alternative?"

Often with laughter, he gave me a positive perspective. "You're going to be okay, no matter how hard life seems," But he also pointed out more than once, "You're the author of your own misery." He convinced me I needed to grow and change and not blame anyone else for what I felt inside.

Pete and Gerry taught me:

Recalibrate your perspective. Gerry and Pete have long since passed, but their influence lives on every day in how I view my work, others, and myself. Their impact led me to develop a high school program called Craftsman with Character® that introduces blue-collar students to the world of manufacturing and the skilled trades, emphasizing character development through mentoring.

A big part of the curriculum helps students realize we are all a mess and need each other. None of us should take ourselves too seriously. That doesn't mean we don't pursue a life of excellence. On the contrary, Gerry and Pete helped me redefine excellence as a life filled with forgiveness, patience, hope, love, and joy. This is the main role of a mentor: to give us all a different perspective of ourselves and the world we didn't know existed.

DAVE HATAJ is the second-generation president and owner of Edgerton Gear, Inc., and also the founder of www.craftsmanwithcharacter.org which introduces high school students to the trades and manufacturing, while developing character and soft skills. He is the author of *Good Work: How Blue Collar Business Can Change Lives, Communities, and the World.*

Chapter 35
Flight Suit by Vernice "FlyGirl" Armour

People ask me:

"Who was your mentor?"

I didn't have *a* mentor. I had an entire *squadron* of mentors!

The best way I can describe it is this: look at a pilot's flight suit, each one is covered in patches; stories, scars, lessons learned, tribes, a moment, missions accomplished.

Mine? It's patched with people.

Some patches were sewn on early. My parents divorced when I was three. Mom married Clarence when I was six. I still remember the day I asked if I could call him Dad (I only knew him as Dad).

My father, Gaston, married Gwen when I was eight.

So, I've always said I am blessed to have two sets of parents when some people don't have any. Each parent is special and different, leaving their unique mark on me.

Mom. Obsessed with appearances and keeping up with the Joneses. It nudged me in the opposite direction and taught me fast. *Approvals are overrated. Authenticity is everything.*

DadC. Marine. Three tour Vietnam vet. Former running back for an NFL team. Hustle, hustle, hustle…take fast action!

Tough as they come. He taught me to stand my ground, fists up, voice strong. He'd throw up his fists and shout, "Hit them! Hit them!" It wasn't about violence; it was about power. *Never fold. Never flinch.* That patch is my spine.

Gwen. A whole different vibe. Rocked leopard print when the world was still in gray. Her life motto: Life is short. *Go live.* That mindset---patch---helped me when people raised eyebrows at my choices. *"You had your life. Now watch me live mine."*

DadG. He was the philosopher of the crew. Twenty-four years in the Army and retired as a major. Taught me to stay focused on the long goal. To dream. To think.

I'll never forget the day we sat at Grandmother Armour's kitchen table. I must've been six or seven. He pulled out a napkin and drew a circle.

"The world," he said, "is built on knowledge. If knowledge were a pie and there were three pieces, what do you think is the first piece? He gave us a hint:

"You know what you know. What's another one?"

I said, *"You know what you **don't** know."*

That's right!

My brother jumped in, *"You don't know what you don't know!"*

I was totally irritated that he guessed it (I mean it WAS a competition!) and totally blown away by the concept. It was another patch, one that I've never forgotten.

When I became a police officer, my Lieutenant (Lou) was a tough and kind Black man. No sugarcoating. He broke me down, built me up and then stood back and watched me fly. I'll always remember Lou.

The Marines? Whole new battlefield.

While I was going through the recruiting process, my recruiting officer let me know that if I made it, I would be the first Black woman to become a pilot in the Marines. #MindBlown!!! To give me a little motivation, he gave me an article, *"Are You the One?"* written by General Stanley.

One of the toughest hurdles to becoming a pilot is passing the written flight test. The first time I took it, I failed by a few points. The pressure was on. Crushed the second test. This same officer continued to invest in my success. He and his girlfriend even drove me from

Nashville to Pensacola so I could take my flight physical. One "waiver for low iron later," I passed and overcame another major hurdle!

All that was left was to submit my packet to Officer Candidate School. Women could only apply once a year. I didn't get accepted and I was crushed. Eighty-eight percent never apply again, but twelve percent do. I was part of that twelve percent the next year, applied and didn't get accepted. Third time is a charm, so I applied again---and didn't get accepted! ***The fourth year***, I know they were thinking, "This person is crazy and not going away!" They were right, and I was accepted. I graduated #1 in my class and had the highest score of the previous 200 students to graduate from flight school. Getting through flight school, I constantly thought about my DadC and DadG and how they taught me to be resilient, tough, and focused on the goal. Mission accomplished and patch earned.

After the Marines, I entered a whole new world of professional speaking. It was tough at first. I started a business and didn't have a clue about how to run one!

I didn't glide; I crashed.

My mortgage was past due. No keynotes booked and no money coming in.

I called around to my contacts and called Larry Allston. I explained my situation and he said, "Vernice, go to Atlanta to that business conference you attended last year, where you decided to depart the Marine Corps and people said they would book you to speak. Go again and you can stay at my place the night before, which is on the way. You'll meet the right people."

So, I said yes. Once I arrived in Atlanta, I decided to sleep in my truck, eat off the dollar menu, and do the hallway hustle because I definitely didn't have the money to get into the conference.

I showed up, no registration, no clue. All I could hear was Larry's voice, "Just get there. You got this." He knew the power was in showing up...and that I'd meet the right people.

Then, I heard someone say my name.

"Captain Armour, we had no clue you were coming! A speaker canceled at the last minute. Can you fill in? And don't worry, we'll take care of your registration and hotel!"

There I was, a speaker for the conference.

Within thirty days, checks from Fortune 500 companies were deposited into my business checking account.

Just show up. Another patch earned from Larry's encouragement and DadC's hustle, hustle philosophy.

My mentors taught me:

Sew on patches of belief onto someone else's flight suit. My mentors stitched lessons of courage and belief into my flight suit. I honor them by helping others, many of whom are aspiring speakers. A few years ago, one of my speaking mentees sent me a text: "I took your advice and lost everything." My stomach dropped. Then another message came through. "Thank goodness. I lost the negatives in my life and now have a thriving business, a great relationship with kids, and a home. Thanks for helping me make my Gutsy Move."

Stop looking for one, magical mentor. There's something to learn from *everyone,* especially those who aren't just like you. Mentorship comes in all forms: big, small, formal, informal.

One conversation. One moment. One spark.

That's how you build your flight suit.

One patch at a time.

VERNICE "FLYGIRL" ARMOUR went from Marine and America's First African American Female Combat Pilot, making 55,000 dollars, to entrepreneur breaking six-figures in her first year of business and seven-figures in four. Featured on CNN, The Oprah Winfrey Show and others, FlyGirl is an internationally recognized speaker.

Chapter 36
Year of the Ox by Lay Tin Ooi

"Oh, Lay Tin is in her black IMU T-shirt and pants with her suitcase in tow. She's off for her roadshows again!"

Early in my career, in my early thirties, I had the privilege of working under a remarkable leader, Dr. Mei Ling Young. As Head of Marketing & Communications, I traveled quite a bit from Malaysia to promote the International Medical University's medical and pharmacy programs.

Dr. Young, the Executive Director, wasn't just my boss, but a guide who shaped my journey in ways I never imagined. At a time when I was balancing the challenges of a growing career and a young family, she saw potential in me I hadn't fully recognized in myself.

"I'm sending you abroad," she announced one day, "to learn from our counterparts in leading medical universities in the UK, U.S., Canada, Australia and New Zealand. You'll create a commemorative book for IMU's tenth anniversary." This was to be an enormous task gathering congratulatory messages from twenty-seven partner universities plus building collaboration and growth opportunities.

"I want you to learn from the best. Go sharpen your axe." This metaphorical call to action was her repeated reminder to continuously hone my skills, to refine my craft, and to strive for excellence in all endeavors. "Like a blacksmith tending to a precious tool, you must invest time and effort into self-improvement and the relentless pursuit of mastery." Those experiences abroad opened my eyes to global best practices, new strategies, and innovative approaches in marketing, communications, student admissions, and alumni management.

Soon she promoted me to Head of Division, Marketing & Communications, Admissions and Student Affairs of the IMU. Never anxious meeting with her, I felt at ease with our work discussions. She valued my insights, listening attentively when I proposed improvements, and encouraged me to refine my ideas giving me the confidence to contribute meaningfully to our organization.

"We share the Chinese zodiac sign, the year of the Ox," she said one day, "though twelve years apart. The Ox represents strength, determination, and resilience, traits we both embody." Our shared sign created an unspoken understanding between us, shaping a professional relationship built on reliability, loyalty and a strong work ethic. Like two Oxen steadily moving forward, we worked with a shared sense of purpose, navigating challenges and opportunities with mutual respect and intuition.

Dr. Young taught me:

Sharpen Your Axe. Dr Young's mentorship extended beyond professional development; it was about trust, encouragement, and genuine investment in someone's future. She showed me what it meant to be a great leader, and her example continues to inspire me to believe in someone's potential. I contribute pro-bono on The Mentoring Club platform based in Berlin. My latest mentee was a young lady from Brazil who wanted to understand more about pursuing a career in Public Relations. Dr. Young's wisdom echoed as I guided her to develop a trusting relationship with her boss and gain clarity on company's direction. Next, I'm joining a group of people on an inaugural Mentors' Xchange in Kuala Lumpur. Perhaps the greatest legacy lies not in the accolades or accomplishments but in the enduring bond forged between two individuals united by a shared vision and a mutual commitment to excellence.

LAY TIN OOI is a Malaysian marketing strategist, accredited corporate trainer, mentor and higher education specialist with over thirty-five years of experience. She drives global branding, public relations, and growth in the private higher education industry. She's committed to practical leadership, lifelong learning, and meaningful impact.

Chapter 37
The Ripple Effect by Ginger Clayton

"Would you like to help me with a diaper drive?" Eileen Rogers asked as we chatted at a local business community event. Her reputation had preceded her. I knew she was a powerhouse... successful, sharp, and intentional. But what drew me in was her calm, grounded presence.

"I'd love to," I answered without hesitation.

She had no idea how this invitation struck a deeply personal chord. Decades earlier, I was a young, divorced, single mom in college, working hard to build a future for myself and my baby. One morning, as I scrambled out the door with a bookbag slung over one shoulder and a diaper bag over the other, I discovered I didn't have enough diapers. No diapers meant no childcare, and no childcare meant I couldn't attend class or work that day. I was terrified. Then, someone pointed me to the Diaper Bank of Southern Arizona, where I received a package of desperately needed diapers. That small act made a massive difference in that moment, which stuck with me forever.

Eileen knew of my interest in community work and my growing desire to make a difference beyond the boardroom. So, when she invited me into that first diaper drive, it felt like more than just giving back; it felt like coming full circle.

Eileen didn't just include me in that effort; she empowered me within it.

She encouraged me to join a CEO coaching group, where I grew as a leader with intention and purpose. She saw something in me that I hadn't seen in myself. She nurtured it and let it grow on its own terms. Never pushing or judging, only inviting and supporting.

She seemed to have a rare ability to hold space for both ambition and balance, something I was desperately craving at the time. Like many entrepreneurs, I subscribed to the belief that burnout was just part of the job. I pushed hard to grow my business, constantly chasing the next milestone and sacrificing my personal life in the process. I hadn't yet realized that success didn't have to come at the cost of my sanity — or my values. But Eileen knew. And she made it her mission to show me another way.

"Remember," she cautioned, "to never let the pursuit of giving back interfere with what matters most…your peace, your time with family, and your joy in the journey. Balance isn't a myth; it's a choice we make, again and again with intention." Watching her navigate her own life … prioritizing her loved ones, her wellness, and her values… showed me that it's possible to lead in both business and life without losing yourself in the process.

Mentorship is often talked about in the context of business strategy, networking, or skill-building, and yes, Eileen offered plenty of wisdom in those areas. But what made her mentorship life-changing was that it was holistic. She mentored the whole me, not just the entrepreneur but also the mother, the friend, and the community member. She reminded me that success is measured not just by revenue but also by relationships, impact, and joy. Because of Eileen, I've built a life I love, one that is rich in family time, business success, and meaningful service to others.

Eileen taught me:

Be the person you needed to be when you were younger. This favorite quote from Eileen helped me see the ripple effects of her mentorship everywhere, especially in myself. I see the version of me Eileen believed in all along. Eileen was that person for me, not only because I was young in years but because I was young in knowing how to live fully. She helped me recognize that philanthropy wasn't just something I could support; it was something I could shape. I try to carry her example forward in everything I do, whether I'm mentoring someone, running my business, or packing diaper donations.

Yes, diaper donations. With Eileen's guidance, I eventually took the reins of the diaper drive she had founded and established the Diaper Bank of Central Arizona. This nonprofit provides over one million diapers annually to local families in need. I see the ripple effects of her mentorship in the parents who receive our diapers and breathe a little easier. In the volunteers who now lead with passion and purpose. In my business, which is thriving without demanding every ounce of me. And in my family because I'm fully present for the moments that matter.

GINGER CLAYTON, CEO of Elontec, leads Arizona's top firm for commercial furniture, moving, and technology solutions. Recognized nationally for entrepreneurial leadership and community impact, she also founded the Diaper Bank of Central AZ to serve families in need. Ginger is passionate about helping others move forward—professionally and personally.

Chapter 38
The Power of One Person
by Kanimozhi Sivakumaran

"Hello America!" I arrived in the United States at age twenty-four, with two suitcases, a few close friends scattered across the country, and a lot of hope. I came from a well-off family in India, but I was chasing something more—better opportunities, and maybe even this mythical thing called work-life balance.

When I started my master's at the University of Colorado, it was exciting and a little terrifying. I was building a new life from the people I was meeting—the food I was eating, to the new cultural norms I was experiencing.

Fortunately, I discovered a program at college called Empowering Women in Business. Think of it as a crash course in not just business, but life—soft skills, confidence, and things that a lot of textbooks never cover.

One of our class assignments was to conduct an informational interview with a local executive. I didn't know it then, but that simple requirement changed everything. Over tea and coffee, I met my mentor, Denise Horton. She is a savvy businesswoman with a big resume and an equally big heart.

After our interview, she looked me straight in the eye and said, "I believe in you. You're going to do big things." Later, she made a statement that still plays on repeat in my head: "Hiring you would be a no-brainer."

That encouragement for a nervous, far-from-home graduate student was like emotional jet fuel. "Would you be open to meeting with me again?"

Her yes made me realize that she saw potential in me before I saw it in myself. I've always been a good student, but I didn't know what I didn't know. At our next meeting, she handed me a questionnaire with simple but profound questions:

- What city do you want to live in?
- What companies do you want to work for?
- What energizes you in work?

I didn't have any answers. I just knew I wanted a job—and a legal reason to stay in the country. But she pushed me to get specific. Now I recognize what Denise knew: a vague vision of success and happiness produces vague, average outcomes.

Then, she did something incredible. She opened her Rolodex (okay, her digital one) and started connecting me to people in those cities and at those companies. I was nervous. What if I mess up these conversations? What if I disappoint her? But her belief gave me courage.

After each interview, she took time to coach me, helping me reflect and refine my approach. More than once, I'd hear the discouraging words, "You just don't have enough experience."

Frustrated I shared with Denise, "Well, how am I supposed to get experience if people only want to hire people with experience!" She wasn't deterred and helped me reframe my answers to demonstrate why I did have the right experience. It just wasn't in the neat little boxes they were expecting.

Then, I got an interview with Netflix. Big name. Big nerves. She was right there helping me prepare. While I didn't get the position, I learned from Denise how to reflect and learn to do better at the next interview.

Since I'm here on a visa, there was an extra layer of stress: Would a company be willing to sponsor me? It wasn't just about being good enough. I had to be one hundred times better to even be considered. Not every connection panned out. Even after a warm introduction, some people didn't show up. One time I was pumped to meet the head of HR at a major company—she ghosted me. Just... vanished.

Hearing a lot of no's created a few days where I cried for fear I'd never land a product manager job. But then I'd hear her voice: "Hiring you would be a no-brainer." That sentence was my reset and recharge button.

Eventually, through Diane's network, I met the SVP of Sling. He didn't hire me—but he introduced me to someone who did. I'm now a product manager at Boost Mobile, working in a place where I feel seen, supported, and challenged. Every day, my manager shows appreciation, and I realize my search for work-life balance was not about the hours worked but about being valued

None of this would have happened without her.

Denise Horton taught me:

The power of one person can change your trajectory. Their confidence in you is contagious and it's okay to borrow some until you build your own. And I can tell you this: If you ever hear someone say, "Hiring you would be a no-brainer"—believe them. And then go prove them right.

Connections matter. Her introductions were the keys to opening doors I could not have found on my own. One of my classmates at college was going through the same confusion and fear I once did. I introduced her to my mentor. Now she's thriving too, with the same voice cheering her on.

KANIMOZHI (DIVYA) SIVAKUMARAN is a Product Manager at DISH (Boost Mobile) with a Master of Science, Master of Information Systems and a Master of Business Administration.

Chapter 39
From Right-Hand-Man to CEO
by Kent Stemper

"If you're good at math and want to make a lot of money where there are lots of jobs... 'My tenth-grade brain jolted awake in math class...' you should go into accounting." That was it. No career counselor, no aptitude test. Just a math teacher's offhand comment and a career was decided.

I started in public accounting at Touche Ross and spent nearly a decade between Denver and Chicago. I'd never go into internal audit because, you know, they were the "dead-end jobs." Ironically, that's exactly what I did when I joined Baxter.

However, Baxter had a perk I couldn't ignore; they would pay for graduate school. I dove headfirst into an MBA at Northwestern, mostly because I knew my business acumen needed an upgrade. I was hungry to learn and ready to level up.

That's when I first heard about Harry Kraemer, then VP of Finance. People said he'd be CEO someday. I thought, *Really? A finance guy?* Turns out, yes. They were right—he became CEO six years later.

At the time, I was one of 50,000 employees and about as close to Harry as I was to the mailroom in Singapore. So, when I got a handwritten note from him congratulating me on finishing my MBA, I was floored. Who does that?

Though our direct interactions were limited early on, Harry's talks left a big impression. He said, "Don't think of yourself as a finance person. You're a businessperson with a specialty in finance. Be the right-hand-man or woman to the person you support." I took that advice to heart.

In my next role, I supported the head of manufacturing in the I.V. Systems Division and adopted Harry's philosophy fully. I didn't just crunch numbers, I became a strategic partner, trying to anticipate needs, not just react to them.

Then came a curveball: "You're probably not the least bit interested," my boss said, "but your name came up for a job in Japan."

Um—interested? Yes. I'd already told HR I wanted international experience, and Japan was *the* finance job. As CFO there, I'd regularly interact with the CEO and executive leadership team. During my four years in Japan, my interactions with Harry became more personal. Leave a voicemail? He called back. Travel to the States? He made time to meet. I eventually realized: he didn't *have* the time—he *made* the time.

After Japan, I moved to Southern California. The division was struggling financially, and soon I was struggling with a personal crisis: a lump on my neck. I was having difficulty getting a diagnosis, and one frustrated surgeon said, "Let's just cut into it and see what it is."

That's when Harry stepped in again. He connected me with Dr. John Wesley, a Baxter physician who Harry called "the Michael Jordan of what he does." Thanks to him, I got a quick biopsy. Fifteen minutes later: diagnosis—Non-Hodgkin's Lymphoma, Stage 1. The surgeon later told me, "Cutting into your tumor could've been disastrous."

So yes—chemotherapy and radiation saved my life. But Harry did, too.

When Harry and several other leaders left Baxter in 2004, I followed suit. I'd spent thirteen years in five increasingly senior roles, all shaped by his influence.

Harry's mentorship touched every major milestone in my life: my family, my MBA, my international career—and my cancer. He led with integrity and modeled servant leadership long before it was a buzzword. As St. Francis of Assisi said, "Preach the gospel daily and if necessary, use words." That's Harry.

Years later, I joined BluSky, a restoration company in Denver. After three years as CFO, the founder, Terry Shadwick, asked me to take over as CEO. Thanks to Harry's example, I learned how to be someone's right-hand man, and it was my turn to lead. When I took the reins, our revenues were fifty million dollars. Over seven years, with a lot of teamwork, and a great culture instilled by Terry, we grew to 700 million dollars, and the value of the company multiplied thirty-seven times.

I wanted my team to "experience Harry" and invited him to speak at our company three times. Like me, people were captivated by Harry's wisdom, authenticity, and generosity. It was no surprise to any of us that he became a professor at Northwestern's Kellogg School of Management and was named Professor of the Year.

Harry Kraemer taught me:

Keep first things first. I write personal notes to say thank you, congratulations, or just "you matter." I'm not sure anyone ever feels like they have *enough* time. But Harry showed me: you make time for what matters.

Build a culture of family. Harry didn't just care when things were going well. He showed up when life got hard. I've tried to model that same compassion with my teams.

If you'd told my tenth-grade self that a quick math-class comment would kick off a career shaped by one of the best leaders I've ever known, I wouldn't have believed you. But that's mentorship—it sneaks up on you, sticks with you, and shapes the life you never saw coming.

KENT STEMPER is CEO of BluSky Restoration, leading the company's growth from fifty million dollars to over 700 million dollars. A committed community advocate, he's shared his talents with the Boys & Girls Club for over twenty years. He and his wife are happily married and proud parents of three children.

Chapter 40
More than a Diagnosis by Martie Moore

The night was busy, call lights going off left and right on our thirty-two-bed mixed unit of pediatrics and oncology. Being the Charge Nurse, I pitched in as I could. As the sun set and the pace quieted down, the team took a moment to breathe.

A call light went off at the end of the hallway. I said I'd get it so the assigned nurse could take her break. As I walked in, I looked quickly at my notes from report: *just admitted today, waiting for laboratory results*. I greeted him with the usual, "Can I help you?"

The young man paused, stumbled with his words, and then asked, "Can I have another blanket?"

As I walked to the linen closet, my heart felt heavy. Listening to that inner voice is so important, and I am so glad I did. I gently covered him with the blanket then sat down next to his bed. We chatted quietly about everything you talk about when two strangers meet for the first time. He had grown up in the area, moved away but was now back. As we spoke, I kept feeling there was something weighing on his heart, yet our conversation stayed on the surface.

As I got up to leave, he asked me to go over to the wardrobe and pull out a black portfolio. He asked, "Can you stay just a little while longer?"

I opened the portfolio and the pages spilled out vibrant blasts of color and beauty. He was an artist with exhibitions in SoHo, Los Angles, and other cities throughout the United States. He described each picture and its story. One was a group of children bending over a table coloring. His eyes twinkled as he shared that in each city where he exhibited, he always found a way to share his love for art and humanity. This picture featured children living in the poorest conditions who had never had the chance to freely draw. He had captured their joy of using new colors, giggling and laughing. Each piece of art took me into a story, a moment, so deeply inspirational. I felt my eyes mist up as I struggled with the words of appreciation I felt.

He took my hand, and said, "I wanted someone to know me more than the man who is dying from AIDS." He knew what the labs would say, he knew the conversation he would be having in the morning with the doctor. He had come home only to be disowned by his family and now lying alone in a hospital bed. "Years from now, my name and face will be a blur to you. Please do not forget that I contributed to society. Please do not forget that my story, like so many others, is more than my diagnosis. Take with you my plea to meet everyone with an open mind and most importantly an open heart."

Within two weeks he passed away quietly with the hospital team by his beside. We became his family.

This brave patient taught me:

Look past the outer to the inner soul. In times when I have met people who are so hard to be near… patients, families, fellow nurses, clinicians, community members, strangers, those who hold deep anger in their souls… I can hear my patient say, "Meet everyone with an open mind and most importantly an open heart."

MARTIE MOORE is an accomplished executive with over thirty-five years of experience in healthcare, specializing in research, quality improvement, patient, resident safety, and the advancement of healthcare delivery systems. Moore has held key leadership roles, including Chief Nursing Officer at corporate, system, and Magnet-designated facilities. She's the co-author of The Leadership Sandwich.

Chapter 41
You Just Ask by Don Yaeger

As a writer for Sports Illustrated, I learned basketball star Shaquille O'Neal held regular meetings with John Wooden, the legendary coach of the UCLA Bruins for twenty-seven seasons. An interesting combination. One was old school, the other was new school. John was white. Shaq was black. I asked to attend a session with Shaq, and at the end, I said to Coach Wooden, "That was fantastic; how do I get time with someone like you?"

He answered, "You just ask."

"Well, how many people ask?"

"Not as many as you'd think."

I called Coach Wooden a few weeks later and asked. His response, "What took you so long?"

For twelve years, I flew to California every other month to spend a day with him. It changed my life. I wasn't just hanging out with Coach Wooden, shooting the breeze. I was learning and growing because of the ground rules he set from the start.

"Don, if we're going to both take time out of our calendars to meet, here are my expectations. Come prepared with questions. Nothing is off limits. This is a judgment-free zone. When the questions are over, our time is over. And when we meet again, the first question I'll ask is, 'How did you apply what I shared?"

I made sure I came prepared with a lot of questions, as I didn't want those impactful conversations to end. I applied and reported back on his advice because I didn't want to be an energy vampire, you know, that person who consistently shows up, asks for time and advice, and does nothing with it.

Various topics were chosen and discussed, one being, "Coach, how do you manage the thirteenth player on your team?" The thirteenth player is often a practice scrub, and there isn't a high probability of playing. I brought a list of the thirteenth players from his years of coaching. He remembered each one of them.

"Don, first I look at what each player needs. No two individuals are alike, and I work hard getting to know each player. I also never hold out false hope, such as telling him he was only six injuries away from playing."

My time with Coach Wooden didn't just focus on how to be a better business person or deal with business issues; it focused on how to be a better person. He emphasized character development, discipline, teamwork, and striving to be the best you are capable of. His famous Pyramid of Success outlined his principles for achieving personal and team excellence.

A favorite lesson he imparted to me was the twenty-first day lesson. His wife had passed away twenty-five years earlier, on the twenty-first of the month. Each day, on the twenty-first day of every month, John Wooden wrote a love letter to his wife in his beautiful handwriting. He'd seal it, place it on her pillow, removing the letter from the previous month. John had boxes and boxes of love letters to his wife.

I asked him, "What are you writing? Is there anything you would have said when your wife was alive?"

"All of it, Don. We often forget to say things we should say."

Coach Wooden died in 2010 at the age of one hundred. His emphasis on values, personal growth, and striving for excellence continues to inspire me and millions in all walks of life today.

Be the Mentor Who Mattered

Coach Wooden taught me:

Ask. I encourage everyone who wants a mentor to simply ask. Stop thinking he or she isn't important enough. And then show up prepared with specific questions. When a mentee shares how he/she has applied their wisdom, it energizes the mentor, knowing it was a good use of time. Questions from the mentee challenge the mentor, allowing him or her to continue to continue to grow.

Show the love. John's love letters inspired me to write a love letter to my wife every Friday. I'm now at 796 weeks. Each Christmas I present her with a box full of fifty-two love letters. It's made me a better person and husband.

DON YAEGER is a Hall of Fame keynote speaker, business leadership coach, a twelve-time New York Times Best-selling author, host of the top-rated Corporate Competitor Podcast, National Geographic's "Storyteller in Residence," and longtime Associate Editor for Sports Illustrated. He is regarded as one of America's most provocative thought leaders.

Chapter 42
Lunch with the Legends by Stu Heinecke

When I was a ten-year-old kid, my brothers and I snuck copies of *Playboy* from our father's dresser drawers. "Look at this!" I whispered in awe. "This is the best cartoon I've ever seen!"

Of course, we looked at the pictures, but I was fascinated by the cartoons and the artists behind them. That inspired my career as a young man with an impossible goal: I wanted to combine my education in marketing with my love of the single-panel gag cartoons.

But, "Humor doesn't work in marketing," claimed David Ogilvy, the famed founder of one of the ten biggest advertising agencies in the world. That created a powerful headwind against my idea to mix cartoons in personalized direct mail campaigns, but I persisted.

I knew that editorial readership surveys found that cartoons are often the best-read and remembered parts of magazines and newspapers. I noticed how people clipped their favorite cartoons and pinned them to bulletin boards, sometimes using white-out on the captions and personalizing them with their own names. That proved that adding these cartoons to mailings would be a winner. I was determined to prove it in one of the biggest arenas by creating campaigns for the largest magazine and newspaper publishers, the most sophisticated direct marketers in the world at the time.

So, I persevered and landed two assignments to create test campaigns for *Bon Appétit* and *Rolling Stone* magazines. And as soon as the results started pouring in, my theory was proven right. Both test campaigns beat their "controls," setting new all-time records for responses.

That changed everything. Almost overnight, I became one of the go-to creatives for subscription mail campaigns in publishing. (That success eventually led to writing *How to Get a Meeting with Anyone*, which SalesDaily later called, *"The #1 sales book ever written on prospecting."*) But it also led me somewhere even more unexpected… into one of the most meaningful mentorship experiences of my life.

By now, I was in demand to create direct mail campaigns for publishers. But I didn't want to offer only *my* cartoons for these assignments. I wanted to form a stable of the world's greatest cartoonists so clients could choose the best to grace their new campaigns.

So, I recruited my heroes of cartooning: Gahan Wilson and Eldon Dedini from *Playboy*, and Leo Cullum, Robert Mankoff, Arnold Levin, Lee Lorenz, Donald Reilly, and more from *The New Yorker*, and Sam Gross from *National Lampoon*. Suddenly, they were all part of my exclusive group providing personalized cartoons for marketing campaigns.

And as the assignments poured in, I found myself surrounded by the very artists whose work I had admired as a ten-year-old kid. Now, I wasn't only working with them, I was spending time with them. I sat in *The New Yorker*'s waiting room on Tuesdays when cartoonists presented their roughs to the cartoon editor, then I joined them for long lunches at the Algonquin Hotel. There I saw how much they loved each other. Even though they were competitors, they had the guiding sense that together they were absolutely necessary to propel this art movement. The more time I spent with them, the more I became one of them. Ours wasn't just a working friendship, but an incredibly special and powerful mentorship experience I'd never imagined. They conferred upon me a unique skill, honed from raw talent and fascination with a very special art form, that, to this day, serves as one of the most powerful engagement devices in marketing.

I can get anyone's attention and make them laugh. I can instantly convert them from strangers to friends. I can lead them to buy anything. My work gained gravitas, eventually ending up in *The Wall Street Journal*, as well as countless record-breaking marketing campaigns, and it all stemmed from that wonderful period in my life, when I hung around with some of the greatest cartoonists of our time.

These cartoonists taught me:

Don't see people as competitors. Connecting with people who are competitors, and more importantly, contemporaries, opens a whole world of collaborations, friendships, and outcomes that wouldn't otherwise happen. It opens our eyes to greater possibilities.

Today, I work with fellow authors, cartoonists, and contact marketers as colleagues. I'm happy to share with them; there's always a feeling of abundance.

Don't hesitate to meet your heroes. It's said we should never meet our heroes. I totally disagree. We should meet them, befriend them, and collaborate when possible. They, like everyone else, are simply people. But they're also extraordinary. And inspiring. And they will lift you in your own life.

STU HEINECKE is a Wall Street Journal cartoonist, bestselling author, and twice-nominated Hall of Fame marketer. Dubbed "the father of Contact Marketing" by the American Marketing Association, he's behind hundreds of record-breaking campaigns for the world's top direct marketers. https://stuheinecke.com.

Chapter 43
A Firm Handshake and the Lord's Prayer
by Lori Jones

It was a warm September afternoon when everything changed. My dad, Kit Sutorius, and I sat in a Chili's restaurant.in Fort Collins, Colorado. At the end of lunch, Dad extended his hand, gave me a firm handshake, and offered me a job. I had no idea that moment would kick off a twenty-five year journey that would shape every part of who I became.

Growing up, I was the shy, awkward kid, the one bullied on the playground. I threw myself into big, bold activities like dance, tennis, and Division I cheerleading, hoping I'd shake the nerves. I didn't. Even with all those activities, public speaking terrified me.

Despite my fear, I graduated with a degree in broadcast journalism. The obvious next step was a career in front of the camera but, try as I might, I just couldn't do it. I was too afraid. That's when, over nachos and fajitas, my dad offered me another path... joining his one-man advertising shop. I said yes. That single decision changed everything.

From day one, Dad and I worked side by side. Hundreds of meetings. Dozens of trade shows. Pitches. Product launches. Branding strategies. And through it all, Dad taught me everything, not only about business but about life.

In those early days, I was the backup band at client meetings, happy to harmonize but terrified of taking the lead. I rehearsed my lines with him over and over. He coached me and encouraged me, but two minutes before showtime, I'd freeze. My hands shook. My voice disappeared.

Yet Dad never made me feel like I failed. Not once. He celebrated every inch forward, believing in me long before I did. He met me where I was... timid, uncertain, hiding behind others in the room. He never pushed me to be someone I wasn't, he simply pulled me toward the person he already saw in me. Inch by inch. Win by win. He helped me rehearse, over and over, until I found my voice. And eventually, I did.

One day, a prospect named Jerry called. We were a finalist for a big contract, and he wanted to stop by and meet our "team" and see our "office."

We had neither.

That was Thursday.

By Friday we signed a lease.

On Saturday, we bought secondhand furniture and spruced it up with wood veneer and upholstery fabric.

On Sunday, we moved in.

By Monday, we were ready... sort of. My family posed as staff to make our firm look more established. When Jerry and his team walked through the door, I was terrified. I felt my nerves taking over. Then my dad gave me that look, the one that silently said, "You've got this."

We had rehearsed the pitch a dozen times. My voice still trembled when it was my turn to speak. But I did it.

After the meeting, Dad didn't focus on my nervousness but celebrated what I got right. He knew the fear was still there, but so was the courage. That meeting wasn't just a milestone for our business; it was a breakthrough for me.

It was the beginning of a new era.

From that point forward, our firm began to grow, and so did I. I eventually led meetings on my own. And before every big one, I'd call Dad for a pep talk. His advice was always the same: "Firm handshake. Look them in the eyes. Then speak." And right before I walk in, I say the Lord's Prayer.

In 2020, I was inducted into the Boulder County Business Hall of Fame. I confidently took the microphone and, with a strong, clear voice, dedicated my speech to Dad. That moment wasn't just an achievement; it was a legacy.

Dad not only helped me become a business leader, he helped me become a confident woman, mother, daughter, and CEO who now mentors others with the same patience, precision, and presence he gave me.

Today, Dad's one-man shop has grown into a full-fledged communication business with dozens of employees. Avocet is more than a firm; it's a family. We believe moms should be moms, and dads should be dads. We lead with integrity. We serve with passion. That DNA, that north star, came from my father.

I was lucky. I had the kind of relationship with my dad that most people only dream of. We worked together. We laughed. We built something that has survived four recessions, a pandemic, and over 350 client journeys. And we did it all with joy.

Dad passed away in 2019. I still lead those meetings, but now I say the prayer with both my fathers... my dad, and our father.

My father taught me:

Build your daughters up. Teach them their worth. Show them who they can be when someone believes in them. Because sometimes, all it takes is a firm handshake, a few rehearsed lines, and someone who believes in you more than you believe in yourself.

LORI JONES, president and CEO of Avocet Communications, is a strategic marketing leader known for driving growth through integrated communications. She partners with both disruptive startups and global brands, helping them break through crowded markets with clarity and impact. Lori also hosts StrategyCast, featuring insights from top business and marketing leaders.

Chapter 44
Now I Get It by David Sevick

I was off to an impressive start in my new job leading marketing and communications for one of Colorado's oldest treatment facilities for children who had experienced trauma, primarily abuse and neglect. In spite of its long and revered history, few people knew about the century-old organization outside of its core groups of loyal supporters. Determined to make the treatment center a household name throughout the Front Range of Colorado, I developed a series of creative strategies to raise community awareness of Tennyson Center for Children and its wonderful mission.

Becky, a lobbyist and contract consultant for several similar organizations, worked in an office at Tennyson Center directly across the hall from mine. Sharing an open-door environment, we easily became involved in each other's work, even if only as observers.

Over the next few years, I accomplished many great things, as did Becky. But my approach didn't always win the favor of my staff or co-workers. My numerous successes became my armor, and I used those achievements as a free pass to avoid having to follow rules or protocol. I often took shortcuts and sometimes looked at the company work hours as merely a suggestion, frequently arriving thirty minutes late and leaving forty-five minutes early. At other times, I chose to miss a meeting or two. "I know what's going to be discussed…no need for me to be there." My work produced lots of accomplishments, even though I wasn't playing by the rules.

At the same time, Becky's endeavors proved remarkably successful. But unlike me, her co-workers and colleagues adored and admired her and held her in the highest regard. Both Becky's and my work were perceived as being of the highest caliber, but the difference was in the perceptions of the people producing that work.

Becky was seen as the golden girl who was single-handedly reforming a broken child welfare system.

I was the guy who got the Tennyson Center its much-deserved attention, but I did it by cheating and breaking rules.

Becky worked on behalf of trauma-affected children because she cared so much about their futures and well-being.

Others perceived that I worked solely for career achievement and personal glory.

At first, I was baffled. Why was I seen as ego-driven and self-serving when Becky was seen as the selfless, inspiring all-American girl next door who dedicated her life to the greater good? We had similar personalities and work styles.

One day, I asked her. I genuinely wanted to understand.

She approached the conversation with her trademark tact and grace. "Dave," she said gently, "let me give you an example. Remember that recent fundraising campaign you led? It took a lot of extra hours and help from the entire development team."

"Yeah," I nodded. "It was a lot of work."

"You did a great job. You raised a lot of much-needed dollars. But you took all the credit. That left your team feeling unappreciated."

Ouch.

I felt defensive and pushed back, but Becky held firm. "Dave," she said, "you asked for this meeting… and for feedback."

Her tone was kind, but she didn't back down. That moment was pure tough love.

I paused. Reflected. Then admitted what I hadn't been willing to see.

"I seldom consider the effects of my actions on other people. What I love most about my job is the recognition... the spotlight. And those are the wrong reasons."

She smiled. "Let me know how I can help."

"I've got a long road ahead of me," I said, "but it's the road to my own reformation. Thanks, Becky."

That conversation and watching her in action became the best tutorial I could've asked for on being a more thoughtful, professional, and compassionate leader.

Today, I work alongside Becky in an organization working to reform a damaged child welfare system to improve the lives of countless children and families throughout Colorado. I love what we do primarily because of the outcomes we produce, ones that directly affect so many lives. And, now I make sure to acknowledge the many people who make those outcomes possible.

Becky taught me:

Courageous diplomacy. In 2020, I started my own marketing and communications company. I was working with a ninety year-old philanthropist, one of my bread-and-butter clients. He was truly brilliant, generous, and... annoying. I saw a lot of my old self in him: stubbornness, selfishness, and a lack of ability to credit a team effort.

Remembering my tough love conversation, I asked to meet, not to talk business but to discuss his behavior. I borrowed Becky's style, putting on my diplomacy hat, speaking slowly and carefully choosing my words. I gave specific examples of how his behavior wasn't necessary or conducive to achieving our mutual goals. To his credit, he listened and didn't get angry or defensive. I sensed his gratitude and laughed when he said, "I hear the same thing from my wife." His behavior changed, as did our working relationship.

No judgment. One of the reasons I sought out Becky's advice was that she is a nonjudgmental person. It's one of the reasons I felt safe asking for her advice. More than once, I've heard her say, "I don't know the entire situation. It's not mine to judge." That mindset has stayed with me. I work every day to model that same attitude towards my friends, colleagues, and clients.

I'm no longer the guy trying to win with my own agenda or shortcuts. I am the guy who tries to lift others up while doing work that matters.

DAVID SEVICK has worked in non-profit leadership roles for the past thirty-five years, specializing in strategies that bring fledgling or struggling organizations into the community spotlight. He also hosts and produces podcasts on a variety of topics and is currently writing a book to be published in the spring of 2026.

Chapter 45
Take the Call by Erin Porteous

Not many can claim that one of their biggest professional life-changing moments happened in a Nordstrom powder room. Now, nearly a decade later, I can still recall faded classical music playing, the warm lighting in the store, and the couch I sat on as I digested the incisive question our Board Chairwoman delivered to me, "Now is your opportunity to become the CEO, do you want it or not?"

Five years earlier, at thirty years old, I was Chief Development Officer of Boys & Girls Clubs of Metro Denver, leading a team responsible for raising an annual operating budget of twelve million dollars, and I also managed a capital campaign, another ten million dollars.

It was my first time reporting to the C-Suite and CEO. Prior to this, I only managed fundraising events. Now, I was charged with the entire revenue stream.

Stanley Druckenmiller, American Investor and Philanthropist, said, "If you're early in your career and they give you a choice between a great mentor or higher pay, take the mentor every time. It's not even close." My CEO agreed and made one of the greatest investments in me- and it didn't cost him a cent.

He asked one of the most prominent, high-powered female lawyers who worked for a Fortune 500 company and sat on our nonprofit Board if she would mentor me.

During monthly lunches over the next two years, she shared advice, asked me questions, and helped me navigate some of the greatest challenges I was facing in our revenue procurement. I was in awe of her success, her confidence, her authenticity, and her willingness to share some of the hard lessons she had learned professionally. Her influence in my professional life catapulted my own success. In a few short years of her investing in me, I learned, I grew and avoided some big mistakes because of her guidance.

Like a lot of working moms, I was trying to balance home and work. She shared a great piece of advice: "It doesn't matter who made the dinner, just make it to the dinner table. With busy schedules, sports games, and work email that never seems to stop, one of the most powerful moments you can have with your kids in a day is at the dinner table. Sometimes it's a homemade meal and sometimes it's cereal, but it's not the food that matters. It's the commitment to being together."

When I was wrestling with an employee, who despite our best coaching efforts, wasn't working out, my mentor's words resonated in my head. "Erin, be slow to hire and quick to fire. When you see the need for change, make the change and move on. Difficult conversations don't get any easier with time."

As I got more settled into my head fundraising role, achieved our annual revenue goals, and eventually completed the capital campaign to build two new buildings, I felt like I was hitting my stride. I was passionate about the work, I felt challenged, and I knew I was making a difference for the kids we served each day.

Years later a couple of friends and I headed to Chicago for a fun weekend. Shortly after landing, we went to a restaurant on Michigan Avenue for a late lunch. During lunch, I saw that our Board Chairwoman---my former mentor---was calling and I let it go to voicemail.

But then she called again.

I made my way to the Nordstrom powder room so I could hear

her. "I met with the Board of Directors; they would like you to consider becoming the CEO as our current CEO is retiring in a few months." I sat there numb, while shoppers bustled by with their bags, overcome with emotions. I was content with my current position, I felt like I was in my stride, and this offer was a professional advancement I thought was still *years* away. I was unprepared, unsettled and reeling for the right response. "Can I think about it?" She could sense my hesitancy and calmly but firmly said, "Do you want the CEO role or not, Erin?" In this moment she represented the company, not my encourager. The choice was mine, and she wouldn't lead me to the answer.

I knew this was my time to say yes, even if I didn't feel entirely ready. If I said no, I may never get the opportunity to sit in the CEO seat for the company I enjoyed working for so much. "Yes, of course, thank you for this opportunity." On my way home, I was still shaken with emotion; among my thoughts were excitement, trepidation, and gratitude. Gratitude that my former mentor had given me the inner confidence to say yes and move forward in this big new role, trepidation as I wondered how I would prepare for this next step in my career journey.

I am in my tenth year as CEO and continue to be grateful that my mentor saw something in me that I had not yet seen in myself. We're still close, and while we find it harder to connect, when we do, we pick up right where we left off. I hope to someday pass along her wisdom to my daughters and to or other aspiring women who juggle motherhood and careers.

Laurie taught me:

It doesn't matter who made the dinner, just make it to the dinner table. With busy schedules, sports games and work email that never seems to stop, one of the most powerful moments you can have with your kids in a day is at the dinner table. It's the commitment to being together.

Say what needs to be said. For nearly two decades I have watched my mentor in a variety of stakeholder settings. She's not vague, and she doesn't beat around the bush; she says what everyone in the room needs to hear, with confidence and honesty.

ERIN PORTEOUS is CEO of Boys & Girls Clubs of Metro Denver, where she has led as CEO since 2016. A respected nonprofit leader, speaker, and award honoree, Erin is dedicated to empowering kids and communities through innovative programs, philanthropy, and compassionate leadership.

Chapter 46
Love and Giving by Val Gokenbach

"Mr. Mitch is here!" the malnourished Haitian orphans screamed, running and hugging and kissing and jumping all over him. My heart swelled as I watched him kneel and welcome them with open arms, hugging and kissing them back.

The medical team I'd assembled got right to work in one of the three cinder block buildings doing physicals, delousing, and deworming all fifty kids in ninety degree humid heat. The precious children were so tiny and undernourished from eating only rice and beans twice a day. Three-year-olds looked like two-year-olds, and the eleven-year-olds were the size of seven-year-olds. We'd brought a nutritionist on the team this year. When we made the kids peanut butter and jelly sandwiches, they grabbed them and ran away so no one could take them, then ran back to us with peanut butter-smeared smiles.

I first met Mitch Albom when I was the Chief Nursing Officer at one of the largest hospitals in the Detroit area. Mitch was and is an icon, both there and beyond, well-known as a radio celebrity, sportswriter, and announcer. An incredible author, he wrote bestselling books such as *Tuesdays with Morrie*, *The Five People You Meet in Heaven*, and many more. Apart from his outstanding professional career, his giving heart and philanthropic efforts included a free clinic for homeless moms and children, a sports center for inner-city kids, homeless shelters for veterans, and this orphanage in Port Au Prince, Haiti.

One of my responsibilities as a CNO was serving on the Board of Visitors for local nursing schools, where I helped guide their programming and provided support for their students. At one meeting, representatives from Mitch's organization showcased his new Super All Year (S.A.Y.) free clinic for homeless and underserved families in Detroit. They asked for help to fulfill Mitch's vision for free diagnostic testing and enhanced quality of care for those people. After our lunch, the other CNOs left, and I wondered *how they could turn their backs and walk away from such a wonderful opportunity to serve.* I stayed to talk to the presenters and pledged to help them.

Shortly after that meeting, I set up a luncheon with our corporate executives and invited Mitch to speak about his vision. "I need your help; our community needs your help." By the end of the luncheon and his heartfelt plea, my hospital vowed to provide all lab tests and many diagnostic procedures for free. For the next five years, I continued to work with Mitch's clinic to provide exam tables, blood pressure machines, expendable supplies, plus one hundred medical staff volunteers.

A year later, I was devasted when the new hospital president terminated my position. This was my dream job, and my departments were performing at the top of their game. I called Mitch that afternoon to tell him what had happened and that he didn't need to worry about his S.A.Y. clinic; I had secured continued support.

He kindly said, "Get in your car and drive to the radio station to talk to me." I wiped my tears, washed my face, and headed downtown. He welcomed me into the studio, and said, "Will you be my Medical Director for the orphanage in Haiti? The kids are in desperately in need of medical care."

I was so amazed with this offer that without hesitation, I answered, "Yes." I was so grateful for this opportunity at a pivotal time in my life to make a difference in the lives of these children.

During our first trip to Haiti, I came to appreciate Mitch and his leadership style. We called ourselves the Detroit Muscle Crew (DMC). The thirty of us included medical professionals, electricians, plumbers, masons, and painters. We slept on air mattresses in buildings under bug nets, took cold showers, flushed toilets with buckets of water, but couldn't drink it because of contamination. The orphanage, situated on one acre of land, consisted of three buildings: a dorm, an administration building, and a chapel that also served as a school. Amazingly, the 2010 earthquake leveled Haiti all around the compound but not the orphanage buildings. Still, the kids refused to sleep inside out of fear that a building might fall on them. A transformational leader, Mitch repeatedly thanked us for our input and contribution to the mission.

Education in Haiti was very expensive, so Mitch decided to build a three-room schoolhouse and hired schoolteachers for each level. From then on, we continued to make improvements to the programs and properties.

We found out that one of our beautiful little girls, Chika, began having neurological symptoms consistent with brain tumors. Mitch and Janine immediately began the process of moving Chika to the states for comprehensive treatment of her tumor. She was diagnosed with DIPG after the doctors at the University of Michigan did her surgery. I contacted the radiology team that I once supervised at my former hospital and arranged for her to be seen by our radiation therapists and to receive follow up radiation therapy. Mitch and Janine opened their home and treated Chika as if she was their own daughter. She was so loved. I felt blessed because, along with a few others, we were able to periodically care for Chika when Mitch and Janine needed help. This amazing little girl, so beautiful and loving, would lay on my lap and say, "I love you, Dr. Val." On good days, we took her to amusement parks, restaurants, parties, and malls and watched the smiling delight on her sweet little face.

After several rounds of radiotherapy and different types of chemotherapy, our hearts broke when the oncologist said, "Her tumor is very aggressive. We were running out of options.

Mitch and his wonderful wife, Janine, adopted Chika and loved her until she took her last breath in their home. His book, *Finding Chika,* is a written testimony to her short but impactful life; she changed us all.

I have a beautiful cross that she painted hanging in my kitchen, along with a shelf featuring her photo, hair ribbons, and Mitch's book about her. Not one day goes by that I don't miss her.

Although the Haitian mission trips for me had to halt, my bond with Mitch remains. I apply all I learned from him to this day as I share his pearls of wisdom with my doctoral nursing students at Baylor University and the medical students at Texas Christian University Bernett School of Medicine. Like Mitch, I listen to my staff and appreciate their contributions to our work. I am grateful every day for what I have, and I pray daily. I am more compassionate and put others' needs before my own. My current mission is to help all those around me succeed and to support and mentor them. I learned the power of this from Mitch Albom.

Mitch taught me:

Spiritual growth. I have had many mentors in my life, all of whom have contributed in some way to my professional success. I feel, however, that the best mentors contribute not only to professional growth but more importantly, to spiritual growth. Mitch taught me the importance of loving, accepting diversity, and giving back to the world. All of this I do today because of his influence. He modeled for me to always put others first, to let people around me grow, to be grateful for them and all I have, to exercise patience at times, and to pray; we prayed every night in Haiti.

The best way to pass these values on to others is by being the best role model I can be and always showing love.

VAL GOKENBACH has spent forty-eight years in hospital administration. She is a professor at Texas Christian University in the school of medicine and Baylor University in the Doctorate of Nursing Practice program. Val led her two organizations to the coveted Magnet designation, the highest distinction a healthcare organization can achieve for nursing excellence.

Chapter 47
Find Your Wingman by Waldo Waldman

One of the most memorable missions of my flying career was a high-stakes joint training flight off the coast of Japan—my first long-range mission in an F–16, deep into unfamiliar territory. Our Korea-based squadron was set to engage with Japanese fighter pilots, simulating an aerial adversary threat. We'd be far from home, navigating unpredictable weather and performing mid-air refueling. It wasn't just complex—it was daunting.

You see, I had a little problem I carried for most of my career: **claustrophobia**.

Most people don't associate fighter pilots with claustrophobia. But mine was born from a scuba diving accident three years into my flying career. A malfunctioning mask triggered a massive panic attack underwater. I nearly died. That trauma buried itself deep in my psyche. I dealt with PTSD and waves of fear that never fully went away.

Still, it never compromised my performance—I'd earned top instructor honors and received numerous awards. But it was always there, lurking beneath the surface.

This mission brought it all back.

It wasn't that the flight was inherently difficult. But I was new to the F–16, flying over 600 miles in poor weather, and operating at the edge of my confidence. My hands were steady, but my mind was spinning. Fear crept in, and doubt followed.

Then came Captain Rob Kosciuszko—callsign *Koz*.

Koz was a fellow pilot with a reputation for excellence. Cool under pressure. Tactical brilliance. A master at planning complex missions. We'd met early in our careers, flown together as instructor pilots, and eventually wound up in Korea at the 35th Fighter Squadron.

But Koz wasn't just skilled—he was the kind of leader who created space for honesty. You didn't need to fake it around him.

And that day, I didn't.

"Koz... I'm struggling, man. I'm not feeling up for this one," I admitted as we reviewed the mission plan.

"I need help."

He didn't flinch. He looked me dead in the eye and said, "Waldo, it's all good, bro. You've got this. We've got a solid plan, and we're going to crush it. I've got your six."

Simple words—but powerful. They got me grounded, centered, and mission-focused!

In the fighter pilot world, "check six" means watching your wingman's back, covering the blind spot, the space you can't see. More than that, it means unconditional support.

That day, Koz checked my six in every sense. His calm, confident presence gave me the courage to strap in and take off. I trusted him. And in turn, he helped me trust myself.

He reminded me I wasn't flying solo.

And his mentorship didn't end in the cockpit. Outside of it, Koz set the bar. He challenged me when I coasted. "Come on, Waldo. You can do better," he'd say. And he was right. Sometimes I wasn't working as hard as I could have.

He pushed me to prepare harder, study deeper, and train smarter. He didn't lecture—he *led*. While others partied, he studied. While some relaxed, he refined. He asked relentless questions—not to annoy—but to grow.

His discipline was quiet but contagious. His humility, relentless. And his example changed me.

I didn't just become a better pilot—I became a better person.

Years later, the roles reversed. Koz went through a painful divorce. This time, I showed up for him—just like he had done for me. I was honored that he reached out to me. And it made a difference… for both of us.

That's what wingmen do. That's what friends who are mentors do. When one is down, the other steps in. It's never a one-way street.

Koz went on to become a one-star general. After retiring, he pursued another dream—becoming a medical doctor and flight surgeon. His commitment to excellence never wavered.

As for me, after twenty-three years in the Air Force, I earned my MBA, served in various sales roles, and ultimately found my calling as a leadership keynote speaker, entrepreneurial coach and author. But every story I tell, every lesson I teach, carries echoes of Koz.

Koz taught me:

Make your mentors your friends—and your friends your mentors. Build relationships with people who challenge you, believe in you, and call you higher.

Help others. Lift those trapped in the dungeon of doubt. Be an encourager, a coach, and a trusted wingman—in and out of the cockpit.

Do the work. Excellence isn't earned in the air—it's forged on the ground. Sweat, sacrifice, and smart prep pave the runway to success. And sometimes, it's a peer or friend who shows you how.

Ask for help. We all have our version of claustrophobia—fears that box us in. Have the courage to be vulnerable. Take off the mask and let someone support you. Give others the *gift* of helping you fly.

Life's challenges may not be six-hour missions, surface-to-air missiles, or bad weather… but they can derail your dreams.

You can't face them alone.

Find your wingman—and better yet, **be someone's**.

WALDO WALDMAN is a Hall of Fame leadership speaker, executive coach, and author of the New York Times Bestseller, *Never Fly Solo*. Known as "The Wingman," he's a decorated fighter pilot, an expert in resilience, and helps leaders accelerate collaborative cultures of courage and trust. His clients include Cisco, Siemens, and The Denver Broncos.

PART IV
SOMEONE NEEDS TO DO SOMETHING – FROM INTENTION TO IMPACT

At some point in our lives, we've all uttered the words, "Well, someone needs to do something about this..." Who is that someone? It's you. It's me.

For the last fifteen years, my work in sales and emotional intelligence often led to discussions around why we don't do what we know what we should do?

We *know* that mentoring is important. It's not a new topic. In ancient Greece, Socrates, a philosopher, guided Plato through question and dialogue.

We *know* that helping others is critical to building healthy cultures and communities. Plato went on to become a prominent philosopher, founding the Academy in Athens illustrating the power of transferring knowledge and wisdom.

We *know* that sharing hard-earned wisdom shortcuts a person's learning and increases their earning. In a five-year study of 1,000 employees conducted by Gartner, they found that twenty-five percent of employees who enrolled in a mentoring program had a salary-grade change, compared to only five percent of workers who did not participate.

We know, we know, we know.

So why don't we do, do, do?

In this next section, we focus on answering these questions. Let's begin.

Chapter 48
Who Me? Yes, You.

It was the spring of 1940 and hundreds of thousands of Allied soldiers were trapped on the beaches of Dunkirk. German forces had surrounded them. The British Navy could not reach them fast enough, and the shallow waters made it impossible for large warships to dock. It looked like the soldiers would be wiped out or captured.

Then something extraordinary happened.

Hundreds of small civilian boats — fishing boats, pleasure crafts, ferries, tugboats — set out across the English Channel. Piloted by ordinary men and women, these "little ships" braved enemy fire and treacherous waters to rescue the stranded soldiers, one load at a time. It wasn't one giant rescue that saved the day — it was thousands of small acts of courage, multiplied. In just over a week, more than 338,000 soldiers were brought to safety.

Oftentimes in life, people don't need a grand rescue. They don't need a battleship. They only need a small boat piloted by a person bringing a word of encouragement, advice, or support. Like the Dunkirk rescue, a thousand small acts of mentorship can help carry people to the other side, one where they can reach their full potential.

There's a wonderful quote from American humorist, Erma Bombeck which serves as a daily reminder to answer the call of mentorship.

"When I stand before God at the end of my life, I would hope that I would have not a single bit of talent left and could say, "I used everything you gave me."

I'm not sure about you, but I plan to show up empty-handed.

Now, you might be thinking, "I don't have a big resume, fancy title, or list of achievements. Who am I to be in a teacher or in a mentor role?" Let's dispel that negative self-talk by examining areas where your unique talents can help others. While this book features a lot of work-related examples, there are other areas where you can provide mentorship or mentor moments.

Everyone has something to contribute.

Be the Encouragement Mentor

You're a person blessed with the gift of lifting others. A generous listener, you are more interested in hearing someone else's story than telling your own. You naturally create space for people to show up and share their goals and challenges. As an encourager, you create psychologically safe conversations, where people are invited to "come as they are."

Your encouraging nature creates The Pygmalion Effect, a psychological phenomenon where higher expectations lead to improved performance. You consciously or subconsciously influence others to achieve those expectations, creating self-fulfilling prophecies of growth and excellence.

Glenna Salsbury was such a person. She was a beloved keynote speaker and inspired many during her time on Earth. Ask anyone who had the good fortune to meet her and you'll hear the same response. "You felt like you were the only person in the room. She always had a kind word, a supportive word." It was not unusual for Glenna to end a conversation with a sincere "I love you." She made you feel like you were unique and special.

She didn't ask people to change. Her love and encouragement helped people change.

If this is your talent, get even more intentional about using it.

Be the Resiliency Mentor

You're like a Super Ball. Despite adversity, you bounce back and bounce forward. You've learned how to use setbacks to become better, not bitter.

Henri Nouwen said, "All healers are wounded healers. They are the most gifted to heal others precisely where we ourselves are wounded or wounded others." Resilient people have experienced wounds and can help others heal their wounds.

This is why Alcoholics Anonymous has been so successful in lifting people out of the pit of addiction. The mentor, the recovering alcoholic, has been in that dreadful pit of addiction. They've got stories to tell: Loss of family, jobs, or health. They also have stories of hope because they've beat their addiction. Their experiences of loss and hope help others dig out of their personal addiction pit and dig into new ways of thinking, acting, and being.

Chris Nikic is a resiliency mentor. Born with Down's syndrome, he was told he'd never walk. His dad, rather than focusing on that limiting prediction, believed and modeled a different message to his son. "Chris, there's one simple rule in life: Get one percent better every day."

At first, one percent meant learning to walk, to eat on his own, to tie his shoes. Later, it meant joining the Special Olympics, learning to ride a bike, and eventually training for something most people—anyone—would find impossible: an Ironman.

Swim 2.4 miles. Bike 112. Run 26.2. All in one day.

In 2020, he crossed the finish line and became the first person with Down syndrome to complete an Ironman. Today he speaks to other kids with disabilities and their parents, sharing his story and his dad's message of resiliency: Just get one percent better. Every day.

Perhaps you're a person who can help people come out better, not bitter.

Be the Compassion Mentor

You've nailed the "walking a mile in someone's shoes." Your ability to articulate what a person is thinking or feeling creates deep emotional connections with others.

In their book, *Tommorrowmind,* authors Gabriella Rosen Kellerman and Martin Seligman share powerful insights into the power and importance of compassion. Sometimes as little as ninety-nine words. One of the stories shared comes from researchers at Johns Hopkins who tested a script for cancer doctors to use when dealing with their patients.

"I know this is a tough experience to go through and I want you to know that I am here with you. Some of the things that I say to you today may be difficult to understand, so I want you to feel comfortable stopping me if I say something that is confusing or doesn't make sense. We are here together and we will go through this together."

Then at the end of the appointment, the doctors said: "I know this is a tough time for you and I want to emphasize again that we are in this together. I will be with you each step of the way."

They discovered these words of compassion yielded less anxiety for each patient.

Still think you need a big title or resume. You don't need an advanced degree to show compassion. What is needed is the ability to care. Your ninety-nine words of compassion will help someone push through hard times.

Be the Business Mentor

Your talent is in sales, finance, or operations. These skills can certainly be shared within your organization. I'd also suggest you take your business experience and serve on a non-profit board. Often, non-profit associations are staffed with people with big hearts. However, these big-hearted people might lack business acumen, impacting their ability to raise the visibility of their organization, fundraise, or invest dollars wisely.

Years ago, I served on a non-profit board where one of my fellow board members was the owner of a successful financial wealth management company. Stan had a strong background in finances and a strong personality. Initially, I thought he was kind of a jerk. During board meetings, he'd challenge the staff on how and where the non-profit was investing dollars. Today, I recognize that Stan was a good mentor. In his line of work, he'd seen thousands of dollars wasted if there wasn't financial rigor applied to budgets and that wasn't going to happen on his watch.

Use your business skills inside and outside of your day-to-day business.

Be the Tough Love Mentor

You've mastered CAREfrontation conversations. You care enough about people to confront behavior that isn't serving them well.

Let's face it, most people are conflict-avoidant. They dread engaging in truth-telling conversations. As a result, behaviors impacting a person's ability to reach their fullest potential are never addressed.

A wonderful story of tough love comes from Kim Scott's book, *Radical Candor*. Shortly after Kim Scott joined Google, she gave a presentation to the company's top brass—including CEO Eric Schmidt and the founders. Afterward, Sheryl Sandberg, then VP of Global Online Sales and Operations, pulled Kim aside with feedback.

"You said 'um' a lot—were you aware of it?"

Kim shrugged it off. "Just a verbal tic, I guess," she replied, waving it away.

Sheryl smiled. "I can see I'm going to have to be really direct to get through to you. You're one of the smartest people I know but saying 'um' so much makes you sound stupid."

As Kim wrote: "Now that got my attention."

It was a truth-telling-mentor moment. Sheryl didn't tell Kim she was stupid. She said she sounded stupid. Kim hired a speech coach and successfully eliminated the "um" habit.

Mentorship isn't always soft and soothing—it sometimes stings but ultimately strengthens.

Be the courageous and caring person who is willing to shine a bright light on our blind spots. I've never accomplished anything worthwhile fumbling in the dark.

Be the Spiritual Mentor

You're a person with a connection to something greater than yourself. Now, this doesn't mean you fast three out of seven days. Or live a life of solitude. Or pray on your knees for ten hours a day. Jan Zabinski, whose story is told in the movie, The Zookeepers Wife, was an avowed atheist. He and his wife saved 300 Jews during the holocaust. I'd say he was a spiritual human being.

There are many great qualities that a spiritual mentor shares, one is the ability to love *all* people. Love requires learning how to forgive. Many people do not know how to forgive and live. Their lives are full of resentment and simmering anger.

The late, great Martin Luther King said, "Bitterness is blindness." I can't tell you how many good people I've met who are bitter and blind. They're not living their best life because they are fiercely clinging to their past life, a past hurt. They are still mad at their parents, siblings, former boss, former spouse, or friend. Their theme song is "Who Done Me Wrong."

A spiritual mentor provides guidance on how to forgive, freeing the person to live fully in the present rather than a past that cannot be changed. A spiritual mentor helps people empty those big backpacks full of resentment and anger.

They also teach people how to live a life of gratitude, improving their mental health. A grateful person isn't an anxious person. A grateful person is not an angry person. A grateful person begins their day with thanks rather than worry.

Spiritual mentors don't preach sermons, they live sermons. Their day-to-day modeling of patience, love, forgiveness, humility, and self-control inspire people to do better and be better.

Be the Health Mentor

I am a bit of a health nut. Back in my twenties, while working at the American Cancer Society, I taught an exercise class after work. Cheerfully, (okay, I was cheerful) my colleagues and I would run around the perimeter of the office. In the conference room, we'd grunt and do sit-ups. No fancy gym or workout equipment. Just one twenty-something-year-old, blessed with too much energy, serving as a health nut mentor.

Obesity is a major health threat in the United States. The CDC reports that more than one hundred million adults are obese. Seventy-four percent of all global deaths are due to chronic disease, of which poor nutrition and physical inactivity are contributing factors.

Take the initiative and encourage your company to schedule a lunch and learn where a nutritionist provides education on how to eat better and feel better.

Start a walking club at work or in your neighborhood. Many people don't even know where or how to get started on an exercise program. "Are you kidding? You want me to walk around the block when a flight of stairs leaves me winded. Have you seen these arms? They're so flabby they flap in the wind." Exercise is a great way to meet people and build community. Misery loves company so when those initial sore muscles show up, remind everyone---they'll have company! Help people take their first health and fitness steps.

At Dunkirk, it wasn't the mighty ships that saved the day. It was hundreds of small boats, piloted by ordinary people to pull others to safety.

◊ Get in your boat.

◊ Bring your specific talents to people.

◊ Be that somebody who does something.

Chapter 49
What Will Your Dash Say?

"For it matters not, how much we own, the cars…the house…the cash.

What matters is how we live and love and how we spend our dash."

– Linda Ellis

There's something about those poetic lines that stop us in our tracks. The "dash" — that small, simple mark between the year we're born and the year we pass tells our life's story. It represents every moment, every relationship, every choice. What will your dash say? Will it speak of someone who made time to lift others up, even when life was busy? Or will it whisper, *"I meant to…"*

That kind of question can stir the soul---or stir up a whole lot of cynicism. Let's be honest. Inspirational words often crash headfirst into real-life obligations. The truth is many of us are already dashing! We dash from work deadlines to daycare pick-ups. We dash from managing teams to managing aging parents. The dash doesn't feel all that poetic when you're already dealing with a full calendar.

Most of us have asked it—even if just silently: *What's in it for me?* In a world where your time is stretched thin, it's fair to wonder how giving more of yourself helps you. Here's the surprising truth: mentorship doesn't just shape someone else's dash---it reshapes yours.

Rick Warrens' book, *The Purpose Driven Life*, sold more than fifty million copies. It's been translated into 137 languages. What's the reason for such success? I believe the answer is in the subtitle of the book, *What on Earth Am I Here For*? It's a question many people ask themselves, consciously or unconsciously.

The Purpose-Driven Bus Driver

Years ago, a colleague of mine was leading a program with RTD bus drivers in Denver, Colorado with the goal of instilling purpose and passion in their jobs. Many participants showed up with a high degree of skepticism. "Uh, we're bus drivers... pretty sure this is not a purpose-driven job."

My colleague masterfully changed their perspective with a few questions:

"Who is riding on your bus?"

"People who need to get to work."

"And if they don't get to work on time, what happens?"

"Well, they may not be able to pay their bills or in certain jobs like healthcare, provide care for patients."

"Who else is riding the bus?"

"People that need to get to doctors' appointments and don't have a car."

"And what happens if they can't get to their doctor's appointments?

"Well, they could get sick or not get an early diagnosis of a disease.

"Who else?"

"Well, I have quite a few passengers that need to provide care and support for their elderly parents."

"And what happens if they are not able to provide that care and support?"

"I'm guessing their parents get lonely or don't have enough food in the house."

That's when the light bulbs started going off—participants realized that their job had meaning and purpose. This new level of awareness created excitement, with participants brainstorming on how they could make a difference.

"Hey, we can be friendly to each passenger. It might be the only kindness the person receives that day."

"I'm going to greet repeat passengers by their name to increase that feeling of community."

"Instead of just opening the door, I'm going to say goodbye with wishes for a great day. One small greeting just might make a huge difference as they are heading into a tough day."

These drivers found a greater purpose and higher job satisfaction because they had moved from autopilot to "super-pilot" delivering people to their important destinations.

Are You Ready to Get High?

Research shows that when you help someone you experience something coined by Allan Luks called "helpers high." This concept originated in the 1980s and has been confirmed by many studies. Helping others produces the feel-good hormones of oxytocin and dopamine, both of which reduce anxiety and depression.

Sonja Lyubomirsky, author of, *The How of Happiness*, shares research around what the happiest people have in common. She found that happy people are often the first to offer a helping hand to coworkers and passersby. Get happy and high!

It's tempting to walk down the path of self-absorption path lined with mirrors reflecting only your life and your needs. But this path only decreases happiness. As Dr. Loretta Scott said, "We can't help everyone, but everyone can help someone."

Look Up

We're so busy looking down at screens that we forget to look up, missing the moments in time where we could make a difference. I guarantee that there is someone who could use ninety-nine words of compassion or encouragement.

Look up. You'll see a seasoned professional struggling with self-doubt, wondering if he or she can keep up in a world of accelerated change.

Look up. Take the new hire at work to lunch. When I moved to Memphis to take on my new role as regional manager, the executive assistant to the president put a note on my desk. "I know what it's like to be new in town. Let's go to lunch next week." I've never forgotten that kind gesture.

Take a moment from your daily dashing to look up and around. Fast forward to the end of your life and ask yourself, "What will my dash say?"

◊ I was too busy to make a difference.

◊ I found the time to make a difference.

◊ I'd like to redo my dash.

◊ I'm proud of my dash.

Chapter 50
Be the Next Greatest Generation

Tom Brokaw famously called them *The Greatest Generation*—those men and women who endured the Great Depression, fought in World War II, and came home to rebuild a nation. They didn't seek fame or fortune. They did what was hard because it was right. Their legacy was built on values like duty, honor, faith, and personal responsibility.

We don't need another world war or economic collapse to define the *next* Greatest Generation. What we need are people willing to show up. People who believe it's their duty—not someday, but now—to guide the next generation. To share their wisdom. To light the path.

So where do you begin? It's simpler than you think: make a decision. Every meaningful action starts there. Will you be the mentor who mattered?

If you're ready to light the path, follow these steps.

Step #1: Get inspired.

Take time to reflect. Settle into a comfortable chair with your favorite beverage. Be still and think about the many people who have crossed throughout your life. A teacher, a neighbor, a coach, a clerk at the grocery store, your first boss, your second boss, parents or grandparents. You'll be surprised at how many mentor moments will come flooding back when you allow yourself space to think and reflect. Grab a piece of paper or your journal and:

- Write down the mentors who mattered in your life, from childhood to adulthood.

- Why did they matter? What did they teach you? What impact did this person have on your life? How did you change? What would have happened without this mentor moment or relationship?

Thank your mentor. If possible, send a thank you note. As the late John F. Kennedy said, "We must find the time to stop and thank those people who make a difference in our lives."

After writing my first book, I wrote a thank you note to my high school accounting and typing teacher, Martin Wedeking. When I was sixteen years old, writing this note was the last thing I thought I'd ever do. He was a tough teacher, demanded discipline and excellence. He was the teacher we talked about behind closed doors. I thanked him for his discipline and high expectations of students. Because of him, I sailed through my accounting class in college and I'm a "whiz" at typing, both of which have been tremendous assets in my work.

Step #2: Catalog your talents.

As noted in previous Chapters, there are many ways to help others. Some mentors teach business skills. Others teach hard skills. And still, others excel at teaching soft skills.

Ask yourself:

- Where have I gained unique experience or insight?
- What hard-earned lessons do I wish someone had told me earlier?
- What do I enjoy teaching, sharing, or talking about the most?
- What hurt or challenge have I overcome that others still struggle with?
- What mistakes have I made that others can learn from?

- How have I created success and who could benefit from this knowledge?

Take a look at the skills below. Some speak to the brain, others to the heart. Think about and write down the gifts you bring to the table as a mentor.

Brainstorm with yourself and others on where and how you can use your talents. Can you share these skills at your company with a peer or direct report? What impact could you make at your local school? Who could benefit from your involvement and experiences right in your neighborhood?

Step #3: Find the time.

Conduct a time (and priority) audit. If you don't know where you're spending your time, you don't know where you're wasting it. This audit requires a healthy dose of reality testing and honesty. (Anyone wasting too much time on bad news?) Here is a sample "time tracker" that will help you gain clarity on what, where and how you are currently investing your time.

ACTIVITY	TIME/HRS	CAN IT BE REDIRECTED?

Now, take time that is focused on bad news and create some good news. Calendar block specific times of the month to help others. You can start small. The key is to start!

Step #4: Get creative with commitment.

Mentorship doesn't require a cleared calendar or a free afternoon, however, it does require intention. A few well-placed minutes in a busy schedule can make an impact. Check out the tips below.

- » **Host a "Ask Me Anything" monthly lunch roundtable.** Potential mentees pack a lunch, notepad, iPad, and questions. Leave the bells, whistles, and enormous PowerPoint presentation at home. The attendees only want your time and wisdom.

- » **Become a search and rescue worker.** Make it a goal to seek out new hires at your company who could use a "best friend at work." Pretend you're wearing night vision goggles to find that peer who is silently struggling with the multiple changes required of their position. Schedule a lunch or coffee, in person or virtual, to show them that there is light at the end of the tunnel.

- » **Host a Veterans Day at your company.** Invite retired executives, seasoned professionals, or "battle-tested" team members to share their stories. I once sat on a panel with other veteran speakers where we were sharing our experiences with aspiring speakers. We weren't there to impress---we were there to confess. One had fallen off a stage mid-presentation. Another watched her skirt drop to her ankles thanks to a faulty zipper. We laughed, cringed a little, and most importantly provided young speakers with hope. Our stories of failure reminded participants it's not where you start, it's where you finish.

» **Hold a scavenger hunt.** My friend and colleague, Carrie Missele, led new hire onboarding at COTG and noticed an increasing number of young sales professionals who were very smart, however, lacked strong communication and connection skills. She created a scavenger hunt where new hires had to schedule a meeting with a senior executive to interview and learn personal and professional insights. The result? A whole lot of fun, stronger communication skills, deeper connections, and a greater sense of belonging.

» **Make it easy.** Most of you eat breakfast, lunch, or dinner. Is it possible for you to provide mentoring over a meal? It doesn't matter if you speak with a piece of lettuce caught in your teeth. Mentees are more focused on the words coming out of your mouth than the food caught in your mouth!

» **Teach and Travel.** Some of you travel each week. Ask your mentee to serve as your personal UBER driver to the airport. I've observed the "driving mentorship program" firsthand with my local chapter of The National Speakers Association. We host excellent speakers from all over the country at our monthly meetings. A member of our chapter picks up the speaker to provide hospitality and ease of travel. The bonus: the volunteer gets one-on-one time (mentoring) with a smart person who shares their expertise while driving to the hotel. I know because I've been a mentee in the "Uber Driving" program. Amazing the insights that can be shared in a thirty or forty-five-minute drive.

» **Add mentoring to another activity.** Perhaps you work out at a gym before or after work. Invite your mentee to join you. You might be surprised at how much conversation can happen on a stationary bike or a walk around the track. Ask a mentee to join you on a hike where you can impart wisdom and improve fitness at the same time.

- If you attend a weekly or monthly association meeting, schedule a thirty minute mentor meeting after the meeting. Thirty minutes, once a month, adds up to 360 hours a year of sharing and caring.

» **Take Five.** The reality is we all waste five minutes or thirty minutes each day. (Anyone besides me guilty of spending too much time watching bad news?) Take these wasted minutes and convert them to *mentor minutes*.

- Write a letter to a person incarcerated in prison. You can be the mentor that reminds this person they don't have to be judged by the worst thing they've done in life.

- Take five minutes to send a meaningful podcast or TED talk to a mentee, Schedule twenty minutes for a debrief—over lunch.

- Take five minutes to make an introduction to a person who could help someone find a job or share much-needed expertise. "Your network is your net worth." Take five minutes to be the connector.

Step #5: Eliminate self-limiting beliefs.

For years, LeAnn and I have taught the power of a positive mindset. Get rid of that negative self-talk that is holding you back. Mentoring only requires a spirit of service. You can't buy it at a store or online. It's living inside of you, just waiting to be opened.

State positive affirmations. Change negative self-talk to positive talk:

- I am fully equipped to be a mentor who matters.
- I have time and energy to devote to other people.
- I look up so that I can see the many opportunities to help others.
- My greatest legacy will be that I am a person who made a difference for one starfish!

Create your affirmations. Put them in a place where you can see them every day. Order a coffee mug or a mousepad with your affirmations. It doesn't have to be fancy—sticky notes will do!

Mentorship allows you to live a life of gratitude and service. Gratitude because you are paying forward the gifts from your great mentors. Service to others because that is what the Next Greatest Generation of people do.

Don't be discouraged if your efforts are not recognized right away. Often, the recipient must develop emotional maturity to recognize a good mentor or a mentor moment.

People who guide others don't do it because they want a small statue erected recognizing all their good deeds. They help because as it's said in the Christian and Jewish faith, you reap what you sow. In Buddhism, Hinduism, and Jainism, the equivalent of this is karma. Your actions, good or bad, will have corresponding consequences in your present or future life.

- Let's be the next greatest generation. Let's be the generation that brings back community and connection.
- Let's be the generation that says enough with the self-absorption encouraged by social media.
- Let's be the generation that refuses to let the pace of life interfere with our ability to improve someone else's life.

Let's be the generation filled with mentors who mattered. Now, go find that starfish.

Colleen Stanley and LeAnn Thieman

Acknowledgements

Writing a book is never a solo act. It usually starts in silence, looking at a screen and a blinking cursor. It only becomes a book because of the generosity of many. And for that, we are profoundly grateful.

A heartfelt thank you to Eric Chester, whose "let's grab lunch" turned into a three-hour conversation that nudged us out of our comfort zones and into action. "Ask anyone and everyone for help OR their story." And ask we did!

We quickly learned that mentorship isn't just something you write about—it's something you receive in real time. When we needed to find mentor stories, *connection* was the operative word. Thank you to Barbara Weaver Smith, Meridith Elliott Powell, and Chuck Smith for cracking open your digital rolodexes and making generous introductions. You didn't just connect, you trusted us with your networks, and we'll never forget it.

When we were down to the wire (and let's be honest, running on coffee and chaos), the team at BSN Sports—Ashley Steiger, Nicolette Lomanto, and Susan Riley—showed up big. Even as both our husbands were hospitalized and deadlines were looming, you worked around our mayhem to help gather the final mentor story. That's grace under pressure.

The old saying, *two heads are better than one*, became our rallying cry—especially when those heads belonged to individuals who kindly read our drafts and then kindly didn't hold back. Jacyn Meyer, Eileen Piper, Alexandra Jungenfeld, and Michael Kuehn, you gave us the gift of candor. You didn't offer empty praise; you offered clarity, insight, and just the right nudges to make our message better.

And what would we have done without our logistics maestro, Julie Points? She was our behind-the-scenes wing woman, ensuring that every 'i' was dotted, every 't' was crossed, and every loose end got tied up with a bow (or at least a well-formatted bullet point).

Thank you to the Calumet Editions team who helped bring this book to life. Ian Graham Leask, thank you for believing in this book. Joshua Weber fielded more than one email from us, keeping the project on track. Blake Cipperly and Gary Lindberg brought it home with their editorial expertise and guidance.

Of course, we wouldn't have a book without our many contributors. With humility and gratitude, you took the time to share your stories and honor your mentors. And what remarkable stories they are---thank you.

About the Authors

Colleen Stanley

LeAnn Thieman

Colleen Stanley is president of SalesLeadership and the author of *Emotional Intelligence for Sales Success* and *Emotional Intelligence for Sales Leadership*, with her works published in eleven languages. Recognized as a leading authority on emotional intelligence in the sales profession, she was named one of the top seven sales influencers of the 21st century by Salesforce. For five consecutive years, Global Sales Gurus has ranked her among the world's top ten, awarding her the #1 spot in 2024. Today, Colleen is leading a new movement to reawaken the power of mentorship. Learn more at salesleadershipdevelopment.com or connect with her on https://www.linkedin.com/in/colleenstanleysli/.

LeAnn Thieman is president of SelfCare for HealthCare®, a proven program that enhances resiliency, engagement, and retention in healthcare organizations. Her inspiring journey began during the Vietnam Orphan Airlift in 1975, where she helped rescue three hundred babies as Saigon was falling. LeAnn is a New York Times bestselling author of twenty-three books, including fourteen Chicken Soup for the Soul titles. Her work has been featured on BBC, NBC, CBS, FOX News, NPR, and more. Visit selfcareforhealthcare.com or connect with her on https://www.linkedin.com/in/leannthieman/.

www.ingramcontent.com/pod-product-compliance
Lightning Source LLC
Chambersburg PA
CBHW032223080426
42735CB00008B/694